STATEMENT OF CASE

ROSEBAY WILLOW HERBE

An Herbe that grows on Waste Land

A NARRATIVE

Living with an illness misleadingly called benign

Lisabeth Rose Fairland

Copyright © Lisabeth Rose Fairland 2014
This book is sold subject to the condition that it shall not, by way of trade or otherwise, be lent, resold, hired out, or otherwise circulated without the publisher's prior consent in any form of binding or cover other than that in which it is published and without a similar condition including this condition being imposed on the subsequent publisher.
The moral right of Lisabeth Rose Fairland has been asserted.
ISBN: 150319566X
ISBN-13: 978-1503195660

ROSE-BAY WLLOW HERBE

This Herbe Mother Nature grows to heal herself and those who are Her Own. Ills, Injustices and Wrongs waste years that She will seek to redeem.

Lives that reach their journeys' end come to the crossing that waits... a ferried crossing, a lifting on the wing, a sudden departure.

There will be flowers, it is Her gesture.

ACKNOWLEDGEMENTS

To
Rose Fyleman for *The Ferryboatman*
Elizabeth Barrett Browning for lines from her sonnet,
'How Do I Love Thee'
W H Davies for *'Sweet Stay-At-Home'*
Walter de la Mare for *'Stranger, A Light I Pray'*
William Blake for lines from *Songs of Innocence*
Edmund Waller for lines from *'The Soul's Dark Cottage'*

Very sincere thanks indeed to Rodney Hamon for remastering some very old photographs and to Kunsang in London for her help in re-typing some of the narrative when I was So Ill. My admiration for her command of English. I should be daunted to learn to speak and write Tibetan.

DEDICATION

To All whose voices are unheard and unsung in the name of injustice.

CONTENTS

PART I

Introduction *1*
1. The Beginning *6*
2. Dancing Classes *15*
3. Ivy Benson *23*
4. The Farmhouse Dairy & Gooserye Cottage *25*

PART II

5. North Wales *30*
6. The Hill of Difficulty, Miss Swannie & 'Goodbye' To My Father *38*
7. 'Goodbye' To My Mother, 'The Soul's Dark Cottage' *48*
8. Into The Dark *53*
9. Many Lands *65*
10. Return To The Hillside Home & Last Farewell To Heidi *71*
11. A Baby Comes Into Our Lives *81*

PART III

12. Mr Justice Parry Is In The Dock *101*
13. The Days Ahead (& Nights) *113*
14. Not A Healing Journey *116*
15. Diary Of Loss *125*
16. Bioresonance, Burrows Lea & Mr Ng *131*
17. Final Days *145*

PART I

Introduction
The Ferryboatman

Ferry me across the water, do boatman, do:
If you've a penny in your purse, I'll ferry you.
I have a penny in my purse, and my eyes are blue,
So ferry me across the water, do boatman do.
- Rose Fyleman

Who is the ferryboatman who rows us across the River of Life? Far away down the years stands the child on the river bank. She to become the Maid and then the Morrigan, who, legend has it, kneels by the river at life's end, washing the stains from our clothing?

Time, trauma and pain leave me forgetful of how long I had lived upstairs in that large house, invited there by Mrs Stronach to stay for a fortnight with her daughter whilst she went on her visit to Ireland, but there I had been some long time, and sitting up in bed, laboriously with pen, ink, and music-lined page I painstakingly wrote down bar after bar of the musical setting written for that verse in pencil.

The change in well-being to that tiredness so endless, and the weakening pain had put at variance, all hopes and dreams and set aside all sense of vocational ideas in nursing years before. The misunderstandings in a confluence of words at home too unhappy to bear, they all led to wondering why I was a daughter so uncherished with an illness that cause them so great fret. Why was I here in this world and where had I come from? From some fair borne somewhere, to leave here, surely something resembling the land or the realm where I had been before.

When I walked the steep pathway, years later, of the Welsh hillside, so severe and unyielding, I reached, breathless, my legs with no strength left in them, the line of beech and elms with the gate in the grey stone wall to the green sward the other side. And here, some way along, the stream where at last I could sit down beside the water and rest.

With relief some kindlier feeling kindled. The land round me seemed more restful. In a little while the words came. They were from the same little book in which The Ferryboatman was found. Those of Mr Greatheart. "Listen," he says and Christian listens, as they hear the shepherd boy singing his song. "I will swear," says Mr Greatheart, "that in his bosom the shepherd-boy hath more of that herbe called hearts-ease, than he that is clad in silk and velvet."

It had been within the first two weeks of coming to visit the sanatorium where my father lay ill that I learnt that of all my possessions, including the very special box of those most meaningful to me, left in the river-house of the grounds at Pyrford Place whilst I came on this visit, none were left. The treasured pictures sent me by Laurence Whistler, most of all the picture of Hero looking from her window at her drowning Leander that I gazed on wonderingly often in my young childhood. Now it all was gone. And I was left, in this land, with nothing but his desolate sorrow that I walked the hills with. In time to come. And to regarner, in the endless years, such things as were needful.

It was a half year later when I made the return visit to this land, that was to be so steep and unkind to me. And to leave behind the villages of the Cotswolds where searchingly I had, in vain spent them. Not to find anywhere to remake home.

STATEMENT OF CASE: ROSEBAY WILLOW HERB

My first journey up here had left me weakened for several days with the travelling. My first steps down the hill were with my mother to the grey-lined street that contained the main shops that were the town of Penmaenmawr. Crossing Farnbrook Road parallel before coming to it, there was then the little footpath steeply down to the street itself, on one side the garden of a bungalow, on the other one of the many little churches, musty but cared for by an elderly couple and at the bottom the open gates on to the road. Across this on the other side was the arcade called the Pant-Yr-Avon, and cutting down a further footpath, a dell of trees known as the Dingle. From under the footbridge crossing this gushed the stream that flowed down through them, finally disappearing again before reaching the sea. To the West was the mountain that gave Penmaenmawr its name, Grey Rock Head. This was the granite face loomed large, quarried for its road making rock that was the hardest in the world.

I had made my first three or four trips down this hill with my mother when for some reason one morning my sense of estrangement in this land was too great, and there welled up in me the kind of lines I always found mindful to think of when returning to the centre of my own being. Those of Elizabeth Barrett Browning. 'How do I love thee? Let me count the ways.'

W ere my footsteps to have love enough in them, surely the feeling in this mountain would change. Some weeks later, I stood with her on the railway station platform, the mountain towering above, and wagons in the siding filled with the hard stone. Beyond them, only the sea and those countries to which eventually this rock would go. Countries all over the world, each wagon named. Surely, if the Mountain were prayed for enough this would heal the world.

In my desolation, I would think of this. In my thoughts and reflections, and in those words in which I often down the years had found my only comfort.

I love thee to the level of every day's
Most quiet need, by sun and candle-light...

I had been a widow too young.

I love thee to the depth and breadth and height
My soul can reach, when feeling out of sight
For the ends of being an ideal grace.

'Ideal grace', how much of this was I always short of. And how much I was going to be without in the years ahead, unknown to me then. Always in the healing minute at nine o'clock, and then at ten, that healing minute kept by many in their prayers, did I dwell on this mountain, and the healing of the world. Of its ewes and their lambs, their brief play turned to crying as they were constantly driven. This crying was to resound in my ears more than was bearable for years. How I prayed to angels for their pity. And for the other creatures with whom we share this earth.

In the darkening winter to follow, the sun would go down behind the rockhead when a sunlit morning had bathed the crisp air, soon after mid-day, plunging the hour suddenly into gloom. This was the time that turned the land into Mordor, that country the brave characters in Tolkien's tale, *The Lord of the Rings*, travelled through.

This was the definitive hour. For the continuation of this tale of courageous and arduous journeying takes them next to the Land of Lothlórien where rest, hospitality and welcome are offered to them until they are able to go on. When this time comes they are given the three gifts of the Lady Galadriel. And of the third, the precious box of earth from her garden was my theme to be made.

The two small apple trees, planted by my father and mother only the year before had already given of their first fruits to go with the blackberries picked on that mountainside, and the rosehips that grew amongst them. Spring bulbs would follow in the coming year and gradually the making of this hillside garden, became the redeeming meaning to help me in remaining here.

Returning to this meaning again and again, as I had to through all the harrowing intervals, when I would have to leave the home, missing it until I returned, intensely, there came the time, eventually when I was to spend my six remote years up at the Mountain Hall, the private residence once built by the quarry owners, the Derbyshire family.

STATEMENT OF CASE: ROSEBAY WILLOW HERB

Here, as I was lying as ill, did I hear the wife of Gordon Wilkinson, after the tragedy of Enniskillen on Armistice Sunday, speaking for the first time of the loss of her daughter. Asked how she felt whenever she went past the war memorial where the bomb buried her daughter and husband, she replied instantly, "Oh, I have to beautify that place."

To her, my heart went out, woman to woman, as I knew the meaning of what she meant. The large sitting room in which I lay, once the open landing of this large residence, had a wide balcony across the roof of the entrance-porch below and black moss covered it. From the convent garden of the large house where I had frequently visited the orchard, I had been given several of the containers in which to plant the flowers vandalised in summer months from the doorway and veranda downstairs. For this was no longer the refined and select place it used to be for the visitors that came. My own efforts to beautify what darkness I lay in were equally vandalised. But this place had represented both war and peace. And I was to keep my thoughts as a beacon here, dismembered as I many times was, in the fear and anguish of the days.

The final words of Lady Galadriel had been, "I hold a light to lighten the world when all other lights have gone out." Here, I was to learn the harms of radiation and its wide implications for this world. And to know its measureless damage.

'O thou, who ordainest the services of Angels and of Men and Women, in that most wonderful and holy Order, Grant that as thy Angels always do thee service in heaven, so they may succour and defend us/on earth.' here

Collect for St Michael and All Angels, September 29th. Found in the Book of Common Prayer upon the bereavement of my father. At Easter 1986.

1. The Beginning

It was a dark December day and the ward was full of cotbeds, in one of which was a little four-year-old girl lying alone. Snow was slowly drifting down like goose feathers beyond the darkened windowpane, in the middle of which hung a blind cord moving slightly from side to side. Presently a nurse came to the side of the cot. Lowering the rail she had in her hand a plate of bread and butter. It was my tea. I did not want the bread and butter, so she said she would go and get the sugar bowl. She returned with it and sprinkled a spoonful on the butter and on the bread. Sugar was rationed and so she was giving me a treat. It is all I remember of six long weeks in an isolation ward in Crewe infirmary. I had scarlet fever.

I had woken on Boxing Day with the pink rash and temperature which put me into hospital for the next six weeks, unable to see my mother, who was just allowed to peek at me through the window of the ward door. Every day she had come to the hospital to visit me, but she was not allowed to wave or attract my attention to let me know she was there in case I was upset, for my baby brother had been born and I was highly infectious.

I had been allowed to take my two Grey Rabbit books with me into hospital that had been in my Christmas stocking, and a red drawstring purse. I tried, vainly, when it was time to leave and go home from the ward, to hide my red drawstring purse up my sleeve and cried to leave my Grey Rabbit books, but I was allowed to take none of them home. Two more books were bought for me and I was bought another little red purse.

I was home in time for my birthday and I was not to be poorly again until I was eight years old. My next contact with illness then was the measles.

* * *

We had moved into a large, cold house at the time my baby brother was born, and I used to sit on the hearth trying to warm my back which always ached. The house was opposite an orchard where I used to go for plums for my mother and we had apple trees in our garden, beyond which were the fields where we used to pick blackberries. Then there would be jam-making and I would stand on a stool to reach to stir with a wooden spoon in the brown enamel preserving pan as the jam bubbled away. Then it would go into the warmed jars ready to line the shelves in the pantry and keep through the winter.

I was general helpmeet round the house. Cleaning things would be kept in the glory hole under the stairs with the vacuum cleaner, macs and wellingtons and it was where I would go when things had to be put away, and I would sit on the vacuum cleaner and sing my songs without the light on in the dark. My repertoire was the songs off the wireless.

"I haven't got a barrel of money..." My favourite lines I would sing over and over again... in the garden... on my bike...

We'll be walking along, singing a song,
Side by side.

My dad used to use the glory hole as well to develop the films off our black and white box camera, and I was always snapping, taking pictures in the garden, or the fields beyond

There were also seven tall poplars opposite, which I used to put into order of size as I lay in bed before I went to sleep. I played happily despite my chest pains which would come on like a severe form of stitch, constricting my breathing, and my aching legs of earlier childhood didn't prevent me from walking to school and taking my little brother when he was old enough.

The measles were followed by the mumps, and the mumps were followed by chickenpox, and I finally got whooping cough during the winter next to come. I whooped for the next two winters after that.

At school we had one afternoon a week doing gardening. I loved this. My mother had given me my own garden already by the flowering currant bush just outside our kitchen window. I had stuck some flowers along little paths that I had made with moss from the engraved letters in our driveway, and put a little mirror in for a pond. Then my little brother ran his cars all over it, so my mother gave me a packet of seeds and helped me to sow them.

One day we learnt we were to have to move from our house and a large pantechnicon van pulled up our driveway over the letters engraved in the stonework. This was an adventure that had not happened to us before. The concept that we were leaving behind the lane, the orchard, the fields and my school, my music teacher, and the village choir who gave their summer performances in Wistaston Memorial Hall never occurred to us. There was no looking back to say 'goodbye' when I was 10 and half years old.

Only when we arrived at a grey pebble-dashed semi-detached house in Russell Road, did my heart sink. This was to be where we were to live. I looked down a grey road at other similar grey houses. It seemed the corner house of Thornash Road we were to have moved into had been bought by somebody else. One lunchtime about a year later however (or so it seemed), the retired couple who were leaving this house rang the doorbell. Their sale, they said, had fallen through. They were retired gardeners from a local nursery and were going to live near their son. We were duly able to move into a nicer and less depressing house.

The piano had arrived when I was six years old and my grandfather had sat down at it for me. I watched at his side as he

STATEMENT OF CASE: ROSEBAY WILLOW HERB

played asking again and again in eager delight, "Play it again to me, play it again. Can I play it, can I play?"

Together with a few other pieces of furniture which came to us from my grandparents' home, the piano had arrived as they were going to move. The small terraced cottage where they were going to live near my aunty Mary held no room for them. And the piano had come to me. My grandfather promised to get me some music, and true to this, a copy eventually arrived of that piece he had sat down to play, from memory. On the front cover was a lady in a dancing dress with a gentleman in tails, and the piece was the title song from the film *No, No, Nanette* with Anna Neagle and Fred Astaire.

'I want to be happy,
But I can't be happy,
Unless I make you happy too...' it went.

That was the essence of my childhood in simple happy ways. Happiness, I realised, essentially inside one. And a happiness to last for the first ten and a half years, until we left the house, and the lane in which they had been spent.

We moved to this house when I was nearly four, and one of the first things I remember was being told I had my baby brother, and the doctor asking me in the bedroom if I was pleased. And for about three years after that I ran up and down stairs for my mother. bringing, fetching, doing anything my mother needed to do, as she recovered a second time, from a birth which was as complicated as the first was. We had a weekly delivery of groceries and coal, but we also used to get the bus and go into the town where my mother would call in at Chesters, and I would be sat on the counter there with my tired legs. A visit to the food office entitled us to two bottles of orange-juice and cod-liver oil, and my legs would ache and ache helping to push the pram, and then the pushchair with my brother in it and shopping underneath.

Presently I started school, and my little brother would wait each day for me to come home, often with earache which tearfully often troubled him. It was not a joy to him when he was old enough to start school and go with me, however. I wonder what happened in those first few school days, for he did not want to go any more. Sobbing fits of tears would accompany leaving the house, and he would strain at my hand as my mother waved from the doorway, saying, "I don't want to go... I don't want to go!"

How I have wished since, through all these years, he was never made to, and that I had not insistently pulled him along. Time and distance change one's perceptions, and whereas at the time it seemed so necessary that he went along, it seems looking back, so necessary that he wasn't forced into something, at the age of just under five, he did not want to do. I believe insistently that I am right now, and that my wisdom at eight and a half years old was wrong.

Instead of him crying at my leaving him behind, he was crying that he was being taken with me. In another two years time, we were going to a different school, and the gateway closed on the childhood years so happily spent. What had seemed a great adventure meant never a backward turn or thought of regret at what was being left behind. There was no goodbye, but a very different future to face.

To move from the country childhood of my Cheshire county, down to the south where my grandfather had found employment prospects for my father where there was a welcome for his skills, was very suburban by contrast, and an intense and severe depression filled me. The saying goes, 'being in one's element'. This was a complete change, and a grey one. I looked down the street from the garden gate at grey looking houses. Grey emptiness filled me. I had found myself completely 'out of my element'. The initial tasks of unpacking crockery and bedding and all essential items with my father done, we awaited the arrival of my mother and brother who were following on. I recovered a kind of happiness of sorts. In a year we moved to our second house round the corner. We renamed the house with the name Chellowdene, which had been carved into the driveway of the home we had left. We were to stay there, or my mother and father were, for twenty more years.

There had been a kindly couple next to us in Russell Road, however. Mr Leat gave me some sweetpea seedlings to plant, and he gave them to me every year.

We had to get the bus to Maybury School. There were no places in the local village school, until I had to sit for the 11-plus. They made a place for my brother that September and I went to Goldsworth School on my bike each day. While at Maybury, however, I had been seen by a doctor because of worsening backache. I had to go three times a week for that year to the hospital for physiotherapy which was painful and tiring and did no good, so it was ended. I was better without these visits. I developed very cold legs and felt the cold in my face as well suffering from a neuralgia which had not troubled me before. There was a difference in the county we lived in with its thick winter fogs that lay in the clay Thames Basin, and the crisp clear frost of Cheshire, situated near the salt mines of Nantwich. Our milkman used to come with a horse and the air steamed from his nostrils on winter mornings as we took a piece of toast to give him on the flat of our hands. The horses in the fields at haymaking, were the same as on the packets of Mornflakes Oats, Bonny and the other two. Two milk churns would be on the back of the cart and we would have a jugful and two bottled pints. I missed the horses when we went. I missed the fields. And I missed the lane . I missed everything about the village, *as I do to this day.*

* * *

My back pain continued at Goldsworth. And then at the end of my second year I was asked if I wanted to move to the grammar school. There had been one place short for those who had passed the 11-plus entrance examination. I was happy at Goldsworth. My school music teacher started a school orchestra and my art teacher taught me bookbinding which I found very interesting. But it seemed the grammar school wasn't to be passed aside. It was not to be the local grammar school however. I had to go to Guildford everyday and this had to be by bus or train. It wore me out and it wore me down. Before leaving Goldsworth I had stood in a line waiting to go into the needlework room where we also had domestic science afternoons, to be given the Salk vaccine for poliomyelitis. As the needle went into my arm, I knew I shouldn't have had it. Something in the whole of my being suffered the most dreadful recoil. I should not have let it be done. But I didn't know. I could not have known beforehand, that it was going to alter the whole of my life to come.

The Grammar School was to prove my undoing. For from the beginning I was unhappy in it. The well of reserve inside me constantly being drawn upon, I did my best to come through these days, until the destroying of heart and hope through my utterly horrible English teacher. This, my best subject, was to turn into hours that were demeaned and remarks written on term reports utterly undeserved. To this, my mother retaliated by going to the school, and with the headmaster, in his study, I was asked if I wanted to go back to my good secondary school where I got on well, and was not so unhappy.

To this, I made the regrettable answer, for always in the future, that I would stay. To go back, I felt, would be a disappointment to my mother and father, But it was a mistake. Once more, hindsight wisdom only, made known the right decision and I still knew it forty-five years on.

To my mother, this woman teacher was loathsome and the undesirable effect of her trying to intervene seemed to mark her increasing unhappiness as well as mine. From this time on she began to suffer from severe psoriasis and frequent boils which would reduce her to fits of sobbing. Moreover, besides this, an irreparable distress of mind.

Fits of crying and remonstrance whether with me or my father would devastate the hour of home-coming. I did not know what to do. Leaving the house in the morning we would both be reduced to floods of tears once more, and I would run for the bus I needed not to miss.

Soon my father was to learn he needed treatment for a shadow on his lungs by a mobile unit at work. Only my brother seemed impervious to this, coming home either with his friends, or going home to their house. How my heart was to break for my mother, and for myself. For then, I know, was the beginning of her illness, not to be diagnosed any more than mine was, until just before the parting of death. More than forty years of heartbreak and constant turn of words. Finally a time would come, when both my father and I would know her beseeching as to what had been done wrong. Where were they're words... Her eyes would be two liquid question marks asking, "What is the matter? Why are you quiet? Is it something I've said? Won't you tell me? Can't you!"

And then shutters would come down, and a reprimanding tone would return.

In my fourth year at that hateful grammar school I fled. Having gone into the staff room to challenge this English teacher about her quite vindictive remarks on my previous term's report, and with my mother's knowing, I found her reclining in something like a trance with the games mistress leaning over her. Up she started and ordered me out. "How dare you come in here?" was her answer to my knock.

In nightmare dreams which followed on for many years I never remembered whether I collected books or even coat, though I must have done. I left with no school certificates, nor exams. And I took comfort only in the words of W.H. Davies in his poem, 'Sweet Stay-At-Home', for if I had gifts, this was one of them, honoured in many of the writings, too, of Kathleen Tynan which I was to find only years on. For the meaning of home was to lie at the heart of me, and that, for my lifetime, was to be my heartache.

Sweet Stay-at-Home, sweet Well-content,
Thou knowest of no strange continent;
Thou hast not felt thy bosom keep
A gentle motion with the deep;
Thou hast not sailed in Indian seas,
Where scent comes forth in every breeze.
Thou has not seen the rich grape grow
For miles as far as eyes can go:
Thou hast not seen a summer's night
When maids could sew by a worm's light;

Sweet Stay-at-Home, Sweet Love-one-place,
Sweet simple maid, bless thy dear face;
For thou hast made more homely stuff
Nurture thy gentle self enough;
I love thee for a heart that's kind --
Not for the knowledge in thy mind.
- W.H. Davies

***

By the time we moved from that home of childhood, Grandad had died, suddenly, in the summer of my being eight years old. He and Grandma had been staying up at the bungalow while my aunty Mary and Uncle Bert had gone for a fortnight's holiday, and after mowing the lawn my grandad came in and sat in the chair, and his breath took leave of him. He was not ill nor did he linger, and the suddenness of his death left my grandmother in a state of shock, and my mother, distant, had to take me on the train down to Euston from Crewe. I remember us getting a lift in a kind post office worker's van across to Waterloo in the keen early frost of the morning, bitterly cold, to arrive at Aldershot where my aunty Mary and uncle had had to return early from being away. My brother was too little to go and my father stayed behind to look after him at home.

We had moved two years afterwards and the following summer Nana had also died. She had been poorly for a long time. Angina had troubled her for several years and she had been looked after by my aunty Mary in the small end of terrace cottage she had found for them at the bottom of Cranmore Lane. For some reason I suffered neither from grief nor a sense of loss missing them, for we had lived such a long way from them, but dear to them I must have been, for on losing my father and mother, I was to find they were with me, and remained with me, from then on in days that were to become more grievous as they went on. And on. Tears could never have been shed in so great anguish as was to come, and I was to bless them, and bless them again, as every evening I drew on the comfort of knowing I was held in their love, whatever the day had contained, whatever courage had had to be found.

And there was courage endlessly to be summoned.

2. Dancing Classes

While still at Goldsworth School I had started to play for a local dancing teacher, Fiona McKeane, as her pianist on Saturday mornings. And it was at her mother's dancing school that I continued to be the pianist after I fled from my English teacher at the grammar school. This was the journey again to Guildford, the School of Dance and Drama run by Bice Bellairs was across the river. After a few weeks playing there, however, I became too distressingly unwell to continue doing this and another interval followed at home.

During this time I picked up the shorthand instruction book I had been given one of the visits Lilian and Jim made from Cheshire to stay with us. My mother and father had met and remained friends from the days they used to go cycling together. I taught myself to type and took a course at a secretarial school in the town to get my speeds up. When I was again well enough I registered with an agency and got my first job with a firm called Medilec who supplied medical instruments. This was just a local distance which took me across the footbridge over the canal and onto the Goldsworth Road. The same journey I used to make going to school there.

Within a few weeks I was well enough to travel to London and my next job was with the music publishers Noel Gay at the top of Charing Cross road. Here I was confronted with a switchboard which I was taught now to operate. Within the first twenty minutes I had to learn to push in and pull out all the plugs to take incoming and outgoing calls with a rapidity that leaves me in awe to this day. I was reminded of this induction in later years when reading all about the Bletchley Park decoding mechanism, illustrated by machines that looked like a larger version of the Gestedtner copying machines that I was later to use at the BBC in the music programmes department at Yalding House.

My next assignment after Noel Gays' was an office of a firm of architects. During the first week I was asked out to lunch by one of the employees there. While waiting for this to be served he asked with some seriousness, what did I believe? I was rather taken by surprise but I had recently read two of Lord Dowding's books, one being *The Dark Star*. It was here that I first read the invocation that was to remain the theme of later years to come... 'And Now call on the Love Ray... and send it out over this sad Dark Star'

I told him so, and he said a few days later, on inviting me to lunch again, that he had been to a lecture given by Lord Dowding's wife, Muriel Dowding, entitled 'Beauty Without Cruelty.' It had been held at Caxton Hall and I went along to see the notice still there.

And so I became invited to join a circle of ladies in Mrs Constance White's house where her garage had been converted into the first boutique. I well remember a visit by the Scottish poet Elspeth Reid who wrote a poem about the first Russian space dog to be sent up into orbit, Laika, and how she had been trained for hours at a time to sit in her capsule before being released after the many tests done on her. Where is her soul today in this cosmos we and all creature kingdoms inhabit I wonder?

May she, with the others, rest upon the Love Ray overseeing our world.

* * *

In the later part of the summer that year, I applied for, and was accepted at the Guildhall School of Dance and Drama in the office there. I worked with four other secretaries, and the office was in the reception area for students and teachers alike to come in and book lessons. Prevailing tiredness continued to impede my days, however in the afternoons and I could take no real pleasure in an open air production of *The Yeomen of the Guard* for which I was able to get tickets for my mother and father, aunt and uncle, and for Lucy who all enjoyed it more than I.

I spent some two years in the company and friendship I knew at the Guildhall. By then I had to have another break, and it was with sadness that I parted, on my last day, with a signed record of the Rachmaninov Concerto, with the names of all those I had worked with and come to know well.

* * *

Steady was the doorman at the Music Department of the BBC at Yalding House up Great Portland Street.

It was here that I was to know the rest of my working days before tired illness finally brought them to an end. Here I met likeable names like Peter Gellhorn, who always asked me to turn over for him at the live Thursday evening studio concerts when he was engaged for a performance. And his secretary, who taught me the Czech version of Rusalka's 'Song to The Moon' - so much more lyrical than the English... My kindly producer, Hugh Middlemiss, insisted on writing by hand all the programme notes for me to type for each broadcast, and I never used my shorthand again during the time I was there.

My train journey was shortened by being able to live with a kindly lady in Wimbledon whose daughter, Sheila Anderson, was producer of one of the Light Music programmes, and in one of the lunch hours at the BBC Club in Chandos Place I met Robin Boyle, who used to present the regular broadcasts of Friday Night Is Music Night, to which I had listened for years at the end of every week. These were the heydays of light music and the glorious words and songs of Ivor Novello. By contrast, the music of the Third Programme was in the hands of William Glock, who wanted only to further the avant garde composers of the day who never wrote anything that was a 'tune'. In order to make these programmes listenable of course, there had to be the inclusion of some of the recognisable classics.

On Thursday mornings there was a weekly programme meeting. To prepare for this I would have typed out all the programme notes onto a stencil and taken them to the copying room. There, on the huge copying machine the roller would be inked, the stencil clipped on, and then the handle would be turned until the number of copies needed were done. To write these notes, I would work, usually after an hour and a half rest in the afternoons in the restroom, and go home after the rush hour at seven or half-past in the evening.

With the help of the rest room intervals I was able to work some three years at the BBC until a throat infection meant a fortnight at home. After my first week back again, I went home at half past five on Friday afternoon, waiting for the bus at Oxford Circus to get to Waterloo, instead of going on the underground train. In all the rush of people trying to get on the bus, however, the bus conductor had to rescue me from being pushed off.

I did not know I had walked out of the BBC for the last time that day. I had said no goodbyes. There was no farewell gesture of my leaving. I did not know I wasn't to see those I remember still today, again. Or the friendly face of Steady who always stood by the lift, opening the door and pressing the button (to send you up to your floor). It was not the passing of happy days, despite the people whose names remain memorable even to this day, for I was unwell, and every day was a strain to reach the end of, and could find no known reason that I was so without the well-being that seemed to belong to a former lifetime.

Weeks passed in a haze after I left kind Mrs Andersen to live again at home. Eventually I went to the surgery with a critical pain that would not lessen in my middle. After a two hour wait I left tireder than I knew how to walk down the pathway, and with a prescription just for a bottle of chalky white medicine. I had to walk to the other side of the railway station where the bus stand was and to get there had to go down the steps and underneath to the other side. There had been a chiropodist just before the steps and I thought I might be allowed to sit down there for a few minutes. The window was filled, however with reading books of Mary Baker Eddy. I tentatively pushed open the door, and a lady welcomed me and said that, certainly, I may sit down. I explained my long wait at the surgery and that I needed to get to the bus. I then heard the door open, and while I was explaining, a man walked in, and straight away the lady said, "This gentleman will take you home."

Within moments I was in the car and on arriving back home a telephone number was given to me, if I needed to contact him again, or the lady I had spoken to. I said, "Thank you," and put the number away.

A month must have passed by before I did or thought any more about this, but I felt it might be impolite to ignore the invitation or to just ignore the kindness. I finally telephoned therefore, just to say thank you and to pass on my gratefulness to the lady for allowing me into the reading room. During the conversation I was then invited, if I wished, to meet her at the house where she lived with his brother's family as well as himself. Her name was Mrs Stronach and I met her young daughter, Mary, who also lived upstairs in the house. Presently a visit was planned to go to Ireland to visit her elder daughter and I was asked if I would like to go and stay for a fortnight with Mary, who worked at a children's nursery. I said "Thank you," and duly went to stay.

Within a few days however, I woke, sickening for something, and it turned out to be German measles, which I had not had. My visit was therefore extended, and I began to hear piano music coming from below for several hours of the day. The family had been a professional musical family for many years, and there were recordings of many of the radio shows they had taken part in downstairs.

One day, as I was making my way down there, I met Tania who also lived in the house. She was a dancer and every time she went up or down the stairs she was followed by her corgi dog, named Muffin. It soon became apparent that the music I had heard was being composed for me. I did not know now what musical avenue was to open, but I duly went home after a while to explain all this. From then on I lived between my home and this talented musical household, but for longer intervals at the house. I still remained very unwell, despite getting better from the German measles, and I had to rest for several hours a day. Mrs Stronach had come back from Ireland of course, and realised that from her invitation I had become resident in the household for these intervals. I explained that music had taken over from my original wish to go into children's nursing, and that I had been the accompanist for the ballet classes having not been able to fulfil this. I had been interested in two Swiss doctors who treated children in one of their hospitals by recognising each of the spinal bones corresponded to the musical scale. Presently a series of musical stories and verse became compiled. I did some story readings at the children's library, and Playschool accepted some of the musical narratives that had been collaborated on.

I had, by this time, been some months living between my home and this large musical house, but there were changes to come, for I knew from the beginning that the house was to become part of a property development with others in that residential area. And so the eventual leave-taking came about. I lived on medical certificates which granted me £6.74 pence a week and went into the town to withdraw this money rather than the local village post office. One day I had taken the bus into the town and offered my payment book over the counter. As she was about to stamp my book, the lady said, "Oh, they want this back," and put it aside. I asked her why and she said there was no reason.

I said she could not take the book off me like that, "Its mine!"

The strength went out of me as she said, "It isn't."

Not my property, no, not mine. Not my money, some handout that I was having to live on. I vowed I would never draw on this money again. And for three whole years, I didn't.

* * *

Some time after the large household had been sold I was contacted with the proposal that I could live in London again, to further the musical possibilities that may happen, and that I would share a house with some nurses who wanted another occupant. I entered this house only to know a shrinking feeling as I went up the stairs and was shown a bedroom that I was to live in. The whole house had a smell of gas in it, but it was the atmosphere that I could not bear. I could not define why, but in this house I felt I could not live, and days later I was carried out of it, to wake up in a hospital bed. At the end of it stood a ward sister. Smiling at me, and in quite a high Welsh voice she said, "We are going to give you a little electricity, my dear." I had no idea what she meant.

Not long afterwards, my mother appeared at the end of the bed. Each day after that she would bring me a cup of tea in the mornings, as I lived through the days, weeks, months of a hinterland, traumatised, unreal, and then, seeing apple blossom unfurl, noticing every fine detail of the garden, the grass, but wishing, somehow, I could run and run and run, until I reached the verdant green of pastures that were another world, another realm beyond this, the land that I had come from, that Summerland... that heaven.

In my bedroom I found that unreturned library books had been there for some time and I visited the library to apologise for this. Speaking to one of the assistants, she mentioned my former English teacher from Goldsworth School, having remembered me from the two years I had spent there. She would, she said, tell him she had seen me. I did return with a further book, a set of the collected verse of Walter de la Mare, published and unpublished. From some of these I took great comfort:

Stranger, a Light I pray,
Not that I pine for day;
Only one beam of light,
To show me Night.

And other poems of sleep, and the spirit's freedom. But the days remained unreal. But most of all, were the two volumes I found of Lawrence Whistler, his poems to celebrate the life of his late young wife, Jill Furze, and 'The Initials in The Heart' the biographical account at their few years together in their Devon valley 'Home.

A few days after my library visit I received a telephone call from my English teacher and he came to see me. I related the dismal unhappiness the grammar school had given me and especially the destructive venom of Mrs Underwood. And of how I had left. He knew of my children's work and said I should have contact with children again. I was not well enough at all but not long afterwards I gave the first of a few piano lessons to a handful of children, including a little spastic boy who trundled up the pathway on his three-wheel bike each week, struggling with the calipers on his legs.

I would have to wake at three in the afternoon to start these lessons and give my total commitment to each child's needs, each being different, and each with individual progress in learning. It was through two of these children that I came to believe in musical dyslexia. The ability to distinguish one note from the other on a page of music can easily be taken for granted. And I believed the natural way for a child to learn was by ear. My brother had had a very good musical memory when we went to the same music teacher, Miss Webb, and he used to rattle off 'The Jolly Farmer' without looking up from the keyboard. Miss Webb would exclaim in horror and cover up his hands to make him look at the music which I thought was completely wrong. Ingrained politeness unfortunately prevented me saying so. She did not inspire him to continue his lessons as a result.

My parents put up with these lessons uncomplaining and I look back and think how forbearing it was of them. Just as it had been forbearing to never complain at the piano practise of years they must have listened to. Worst for them must have been when I was asked to play the background music for an hour or two in the lounge of a large country house some few miles away. This was torture, however, to memorise and memorise and repeatedly play over in the evenings at home, a repertoire of popular tunes of the day. How did they bear it? They couldn't. They went for a week's visit to see Jim and Lilian who had moved to North Wales after my dad had to have some more treatment at work. Their mobile unit had again shown further shadow on his lungs. I gave up the country house engagement with which I could not go on.

3. Ivy Benson

I do not remember how I came to be known to Les Allen, so much did this traumatised living perpetuate each day's unreality, fractured in mind and in spirit. I only remember him sitting in our front room one day while I played him one of the pieces that had been written for me some two years or three, before. Upon this he had decided he wanted to arrange a demo disc at studios in Shepperton. But I have the vaguest recollection of any of it.

The next thing I do remember however, was being in his house together with his immensely kind wife Joan. He had been contacted by Ivy Benson, whose pianist had had to take her leave at the last minute from a forthcoming two-week engagement in Switzerland. He wanted to take me to see Ivy at her house and for her it seemed a foregone conclusion that, in view of this, I would stand in for these two weeks. This meant the journey by ferry and train which made those of us in the cabin seasick. We arrived to the snow-lined streets crisp and cold, but found ourselves in warm lodgings. There was, however, the two-hour nightly stand and the challenge of this to fulfil. Ivy was a fully professional musician and a brilliant saxophonist, as well as a pianist herself. For the first week I managed each nightly performance. To all my distress, however, this I could not sustain through the second week, and kind as she was in always taking care of her girls, she saw me onto the train to make the journey back on my own, and to endure the ferry crossing again without the company I had gone with. This, to my dying day, I will sustain remorse over, for I had let her so badly down. I hold her in such affection with an undying gratitude for the privilege that I was even invited to join such a professional group of musicians, looked after by a woman of such rare quality. No sadder memory could I have of all the possibilities of those years, fighting on through the shadowland of trauma still unbroken by any re-emergence into reality.

4. The Farmhouse Dairy & Gooserye Cottage

There remained the few children's piano lessons I had to give, but not for very much longer. My father had been told at work by the medical specialist he had seen, that as long as he was breathing fine oil-dust off his lathe his emphysema would worsen and further shadows return. On their visit to Jim and Lilian they put their names down for one of the hillside homes being built a mile beyond.

* * *

Their impending departure meant I had to decide what to do with many of my things. My piano went to one of the children I had given lessons to. The piano in their home had keys that stuck down, and she had brothers and sisters who always used to come to the door with her, and then come back for her on her leaving, and so to her it went, just as it had some to me from my grandmother when I was six.

There remained my bedroom furniture, a triple mirror framed in walnut, and a dressing table bought from a furniture shop in the town who always looked out for nice things for me. One day, going into the shop the lady said, "I've got something in the back for you," and she brought out a bentwood rocking chair which she sold for a few pounds to me. There was also a small chesterfield sofa with two drop ends which was so comfy, and which I bought for a handsome sum. Eight pounds. There was also my music, my books, the piano stool which had not gone with the piano, and pictures. I also had the precious things dear Miss Seager gave me, whom I used to visit in her cottage home on the Chobham Road just out of the town past the canal bridge. She had gradually been losing her sight, and was trying to make arrangements about her things before she went completely blind. Her sewing machine, fireside table, a beautiful folding Queen Anne piece that she kept just between the hearth and her chair, a set of initialled cutlery and apron, are the things I remember. A bunch of lavender she picked from bar garden and tied remained in my suitcase for years until the mildew of some rooms' down in the Dingle turned them into a bunch of green mould.

All these things were returned to the storage part of the shop where I had bought them. Knowing I needed somewhere to go they mentioned the owner of a farmhouse who was letting the converted dairy, and whose light was on in an office across the corner. Telling him the furniture shop were storing my things, he said I could have the dairy bungalow for the summer holidays rent free, but he would not agree to a longer letting, nor to accept any rent. I duly moved out there to live halfway towards Guildford for the next six weeks.

On moving here my dressing table and mirror went with me, and also my piano stool and gramophone, and with me, also, my dear Puss in his basket. The owner of the farmhouse himself took them there, and myself.

As August drew on to September I became increasingly anxious as to where next I could go. Deciding I must part with my remaining furniture as I could not keep moving it around, mention was made of a lady who had an antiques shop, and who would probably like my walnut mirror and dressing table. Her daughter lived in the cottage at the end of Gooserye Lane. She took my piano stool as well and at the same time I was offered a room in the cottage upstairs which was spare. This was opposite the room occupied by a photographic student, Hugh, who was doing a course at university. Together with my Puss and few other things I still had, I left the farmhouse when the date expired and moved in.

The house belonged to the Broadwoods, descended from the pianomaker of that name, and there were children and their friends coming home from school each day. This meant the house was not a quiet one and Hugh had moved down to the adjoining barn room which they had agreed to give him. Here, he made a fire in the fireplace one night and said, "Use it any time," as he was mostly away in London, coming back to the cottage occasionally in the week.

It was here, in the dark of November that I took my notebook and began writing, trying to describe the illness. It was so hard to define with its tiring and painful misery completely without a name.

Some days had to be spent in bed nearly all day as the winter drew on. The walk to the nearby shop was not far away to get food for myself and my Puss, but he had always known fish from the fresh fish shop as well, and it was on a raw dismal day that I ventured into Guildford to get him some. Waiting for the bus to come back I stood with one other lady down by the river, until numb with cold I noticed the strip of paper across the timetable.

"Have they cancelled our bus at all?" I asked her, and she went to have a look. I cried out "Oh no!" as she read the notice. The bus had indeed been cancelled. The next thing I knew an ambulance was drawing up beside us. Pleading that I did not want to be taken into hospital, they then agreed to get a taxi to take me back to the cottage, but said that they would follow. I wonder who the lady was who sent for that pair of kind ambulance men, and where she may be today? What have the years held for her, I wonder. Her small act of kindness was followed by the ambulance men contacting the GP in that area, John Nichols, and speaking to him about me. He was willing to come out and visit me there and then, they said, but I had to ring him. I did this while they were there, and presently he sat on the end of my bed and said the bone pain that set in that I suffered from was due to a poor supply of the hormone progesterone, and that I 'did not make enough for myself'. He duly prescribed some tablets for me, which were sadly not very effective, but this was the start of the research of Dr John Lee who formulated the subdermal cream that supplied this vital hormone to the bloodstream through the skin. His books and lectures were to become well-known and he was invited to come to the UK St Thomas' Hospital, who had done so much damage to me. If I deserved anything, it would be to have this treatment today, but it still awaits a license granted to be available on prescription, he was also invited to the Royal Masonic Hospital and upon his death a memorial service was held at St Bride's Church, Fleet Street, to honour the lifetime's work he had given to this research, and the wide implications on so many aspects of health he discovered and wrote about.

In the further months of the winter, I decided, with Dr Nichols' knowledge, to go and seek any further help there might be from the London Homeopathic Hospital. On the way back across London the day I went, I decided to spend an hour having a cup of tea at Fortnum's, for the calm and restorativeness the surroundings would give me.

I chose a table in the calm of this oasis and awaited a pot of tea. Within three or four minutes a young, fair-haired woman approached the table and asked if she might sit down. I said, "Yes of course," and learnt that she had been waiting for an MP to give her an interview and they had never arrived. She calmed down after a while and we became deep in conversation. This setting was balm to my fractured mind, still suffering daily from the effects I not recovered from, of my time in St. Thomas' hospital under William Sargent. One of the things that I still don't understand today, is why I made no protest at the treatment I was given for so long, why I was compliant, and it troubled me. Before we parted she wrote down her telephone number and told me to 'come and have tea with her' a fortnight later. Her name was Nesta Wyn Ellis.

Having tea in her flat in two weeks time, she said she had a friend with a cottage to let in Devon. "What you need," she said, "is a change." By mid-February I was on my way down to Kingsbridge with my Puss in his basket, patient and trusting as long as he wasn't parted again from me, as for a time, he had been. Before leaving, however, Hugh had suggested my moving from Gooserye Cottage to a part of west Byfleet, where some friends of his were leaving. This was at Pyrford in fact, and in the grounds of a rambling manor house there were two cottages, a gatehouse, and another house by the river. "I'll take you over and introduce you to Mrs Sinclair," he said. It was

STATEMENT OF CASE: ROSEBAY WILLOW HERB

a day of mist and dank cold, and on knocking at the wooden door and ringing the bell, the door was unlocked and we were welcomed in. There had been a secretary of her husband's who had lived with them for many years even after retirement, and she was to move upstairs from a corner wing with its own entrance and small paved garden. This was what was offered to me, but the roof needed repairing. My things could be looked after, however, in the river house, she said, and duly took us down there. There was a tree-lined driveway to the house and I had wondered if I would ever be able to walk down it. On covering the distance down to the riverhouse I was even more uncertain. I would, I was sure, have to send for some form of transport if I was to live here. Never the less a lady whose children I had once given piano lessons to helped me to move all my things before making my journey down to Devon, and as my mother had requested it, on up to North Wales.

PART II

5. North Wales

For some reason I was not uplifted on this journey and did not have the sense of looking forward to this two week stay in the Devon cottage offered me. The kindly lady who held the key next door had a little girl who ran round a few minutes later, and lifting the letterbox, her two eyes peered in. My Puss made his way round downstairs and then upstairs and I made a cup of tea. But something of an unease prevented me from feeling any sense of a pleasant change here, and instead I found myself feeling something had happened here. The cottage was for sale and had been for a while, this I knew, and one day a key went into the door and three people entered. One of them was the estate agent who wanted to show the people round. Not knowing it had been let for a fortnight and realising my upset and alarm, they left. But I felt frightened at the intrusion, which the neighbour next door hadn't warned me about. My Puss did not seem troubled in the way I was, and walked through the room with his tail in the air nonchalantly and undisturbed.

The second weekend there was to be my birthday and this year it fell on Mothering Sunday. On Saturday a birthday card arrived in the post from my mother and father, inside a letter enclosing their card.

STATEMENT OF CASE: ROSEBAY WILLOW HERB

As I read the birthday message, a feeling of dismay beyond telling came over me at my fathers' handwriting which trailed off unfinished. *Whatever has happened*, I wondered, and read the letter. I then telephoned my mother. He was in the sanatorium in Snowdonia, Bryn Seint, seriously ill with TB.

The journey on Sunday morning was of the most fear-making recollection, and I stood on the railway platform in the blinding sun almost catatonic with this fear and frantic at the same time. When the train pulled in I felt unable to move or get on the train. I was the only one left standing when the guard came along and asked me if I was getting on. Opening the door he put my suitcase and my cat basket on for me, and I stepped on just as he closed the door and the train pulled away.

The final part of the journey from Chester was interminable. The smell of diesel filled the carriages and opening the windows was no better. I was met by my mother with our nearby neighbour who had driven her down the hill. My mother said my dad knew I was coming, but that I would need a day's rest after the journey. When I saw him he just broke down and cried, and I picked up a skeleton in my arms. "I've been waiting," he sobbed. "It's seemed so long." Presently the ward sister asked to see me. My dad had been delirious, asking for me for days.

"He's been very, very poorly," she said in her lilting Welsh voice very different to the Sister in the ECT ward with her high-pitched intonation. "We thought we were going to lose him."

If only I had been there. I would not have left his bedside. I was told we could visit any time of day. It was unbearable to leave him and make the long walk back to the bus, to reach Caernarvon, and then another bus, and then another. Yet I walked that distance for these weeks visiting the sanatorium. Rest would be restorative to my muscles in those days. It was to be years on that this sustainability was eventually lost.

* * *

My father gradually gained a little in strength during that first week visiting and my mother suggested we went on alternate days because of the distance. At the end of the second week the front doorbell rang and on my mother answering it, she showed the local vicar into the front room. Thinking this was perhaps for the same reason that the ward sister had seen me in her room, I greeted him. It was not however, about my father that he had come. Mrs Sinclair from Pyrford Place had telephoned him to bring me news of dire effect on me. She knew I would be upset and had not wanted to tell me herself what had happened.

There was, however, no remnant left of the possessions that had been taken there and left upstairs in the riverhouse. It had been burnt to the ground during the night previously, and on telephoning her, she said that only the fireplace and rose archway were left standing. Boys of ten and sixteen had crossed the river boundary and set fire to it. Seven fire engines put the blaze out. The ground was a quagmire.

There was nothing, absolutely nothing left, not even my sewing machine? Could its iron frame actually melt down to molten metal? As one by one each of my cared for possessions went through my mind, I sank into screaming anguish. My mother had left to take our year-old sheepdog, Heidi, for a walk up to the waterfall. Probably she needed to take it all in for herself. Most of all, what were they to do with me? I was their daughter, on their hands once more. I had some vague illness. It had no name. It had tried and tested them and eventually, for my father's sake, and for his health, they had come to north Wales. It had done him no good. It had left me stranded in a land far from home with its own language. Our sheepdog had been a rescued puppy, abandoned by some children in a builders' hut on the grass verge opposite. With her, the three of them were complete. What was to happen to me?

There was no choice, I knew, but to go back to see my doctor, John Nichols. To try and find a room in a guesthouse somewhere temporarily. My mother went to the hospital and told my father. He was upset, and sent me his love. I saw him the next day. "You must forget!" he said. "You must forget." He was racked, as I was.

I said goodbye to him. Knowing I must make this return journey. To salvage something, surely must be possible. Would I not find the pink glass necklace with the drop pendants lying somewhere in this blackened mire?

There must be something?

STATEMENT OF CASE: ROSEBAY WILLOW HERB

* * *

I sobbed in the corridor of the train as the miles to Chester went on. My mother's parting words had been uncomforting to me. I did not have JourneyCare assistance as I would today. I found a seat in the train at Chester that was to take me back to London and then on back to Surrey and to a two night stay in a guesthouse, so that I could visit Dr Nichols. He was to do his best for three months, exploring every avenue he could when the Social Services failed to be of help to find me somewhere to live, but in vain.

Mrs Sinclair was of no commiseration when I reached Pyrford Place, which, at the end of my journey, had been early evening. She had leaned out of an upper window, saying she was 'getting supper,' and I was not, as formerly, invited in. She asked a groundsman to take me down to the riverhouse. On the approach we came to mounds of blackened bricks here and there. It was, as she had said on the telephone, a quagmire, left by all the fire engines, and no further could we go. I had no wish to see her again. She had said there would be no rent book during the tenancy, as it would make it seem 'more like home.'

How naive could I have been all those years ago! I had not met her barrister husband, who she said had "Worked on the Lindbergh trials," in her first meeting with Hugh and I. It was an endorsement of the contempt I later came to have for the legal system, years on.

I was well rid of her. No greater mistake could there have been, than to go there. My books, music, pictures, sewing things and furniture all gone, including the photographed illustrations sent to me by Laurence Whilstler together with the letters after writing to him about his books, *The Initials In The Heart*, engraved in a glass goblet, and *To Celebrate Her Living*. There had been an exhibition of all his glass engraving, the art he revived, to which I could not go. The curator said on the telephone that I should write as I wanted to frame pictures, with permission, from the book. He sent them followed by two others which included a landscape with poplars. They were all lost now.

I went the next day to see the lady in the furniture shop where my things had been cared for in storage. But the shop was not there. Nor the next one to it. Nor the next one. Razed to the ground had they all been in these five weeks. I stood in the empty space left there. I stood... And I stood. Where there had been kind help such a few months before. Now there was just this emptiness. And abandon. The emptiness of my life filled this waste space. Emptiness. Just emptiness. That is all there was. Desolation in this place.

* * *

I spent the weeks until July between Fairford, Burford, and Taynton where we used to know a lady with whom we stayed, and whose sheepdogs we looked after while she went to Canada one summer - she had taken them off a farmer as both had gone blind. Petronella Erdman, whose Cotswold home I found had been advertised for sale or auction, presumably after she and her sheepdogs were gone. It left another sense of loss. And emptiness.

I came to know the keeper of a bookshop and his wife in Burford where I was welcomed to go and whose garden I was able to enjoy. I had stayed originally at Fullbrook in an orchard bungalow for six weeks of the cold spring that year, until May when it was booked for the rest of the summer. Every day I was brought a jug of fresh milk which I used to make drop scones. Twenty eight buff-brown hens lived in the orchard and one little hen obligingly always laid her eggs just beneath the kitchen window. A baby calf was born just after I arrived and I would visit him in his stall. The lowing of his mother for him made my heart ache, but I was told her milk was too rich for him, and he would get colic if he had too much to be good for him. But is this right? Is it nature's way? I would go and stroke him and he would lick my winter coat and lick and lick it. One day I went to visit his stall only to find it empty, and his hay all cleaned out and I returned with a heavy heart, to weep inside. Both for him, and for his mother. And for his future.

As the end of May approached, so did the anguish of leaving and of having nowhere further to stay. I was, a week or so at a time able to find here or to find there, until by July I made my journey back up to North Wales, this time by coach. My head became sick as the time went by, and stopping again at Chirk for a half hour break, I did not know how to go on. I was to face the same search in this land once again, for somewhere to live, after a while again with my father and with my mother. I stayed in the hillside home until November when the days darkened once more. We went late blackberrying across the hillside and it was here, as the brilliant late morning sun went down behind the mountain, that the inkling of blessings needed was sensed. In the cold of the afternoon we did not linger, but turned to go back and make a warm cup of tea.

* * *

My father's recovery had been a gradual lessening of the sickness each morning of taking the streptomycin that had been necessary, and only gradually did he get back to driving. His emphysema, however, was to take its slow, progressive course. He would struggle to get his arms out of his coat and later, in a further time of my own illness, I knew how disabling and fragile this was to make me feel. And I knew how it must be for him. *9 Years Later*

It was a Sunday afternoon when my mother, leaving the house with my father, slipped and fractured the top of her leg, her femur, and spent the next three weeks in hospital. On coming home, she slept with me in my bed as she needed a cradle under the bed clothes, and the process of getting dressed and getting her stockings on delayed the walk expected by our patient sheepdog. She had never been allowed to wander on her own.

I had fallen off the kitchen chair a few says before, whilst trying to look out of the window to see if she was lying on the path by the steps, as I had heard a bark up the hillside. So, on going out with her, I sat on the wall at the corner while she leapt off up to the waterfall. Within a minute or two a lady spoke to me, on her way up the hill herself. She was staying at the convent for two weeks. As we talked, Heidi ran back down the hill with an anxious look, wondering why I hadn't followed. I explained why her usual walk wasn't possible, and the lady, a Mrs Elizabeth Anne Williams, said she would call before she left to return to Arbroath in Scotland.

It transpired she intended to come back again in a few weeks time but the convent was fully booked for the rest of the summer. I said I would contact Mrs Pollard on Fernbrook Road at Rhiwlas, and she was duly able to stay there on her return. She learnt of my mother and father's disappointment in not feeling able to move back to Hampshire or Surrey. Several housing associations had failed to be able to help them and one in particular had fallen through. Then there was the problem of selling the home in Wales if they did move back. Mrs Williams offered to help in this. She would, she said, be happy to buy the home to visit when she could. Meanwhile, it would be possible for me to stay and live there myself. This, she was making as a gift to me, and I asked if she could put it all into writing. I could then genuinely tell my aunt and Mr Sells, their solicitor, of her offer.

Incriminatingly, my aunt said I had had no right to do so and Mr Sells said he would only take instructions from my parents. I was letting him know, as he had regretted being unable to help my mother and father himself to find a home with the Achilles Housing Association, of her kind offer. And in spite of the courteous letter my parents did receive, they turned her offer down. And not in writing.

In November 1973 two weeks after my mother and father had departed for the hillside in North Wales, I received a visit from Mr Sells. 'I promised your parents I would come and see you,' he said. 'And if there is any kind of help you need at any time, you are not to hesitate to come and see me.'

They had spent a 'good-bye' visit at Ronald and Peggy Sells' house. From Him and his Wife there came a card at Christmas every year. On knowing there was an opportunity for my mother and father to move back to Surrey again, I was left hurt, saddened and perplexed that He was not to be of this help, to them or to Me.

It was at Easter two years on when my father's struggle finally ended for him. He had moved into my bedroom because of his cough and had been ill with a high temperature. Mr Hollas from the chemist had brought up oxygen cylinders to help his breathing. He had previously said they did not give him much relief, and they must not have assisted him in his final struggle. I did not know any of this. I was living below in the basement of Dilys's hair salon above the Dingle. Daffodils under the trees there had been picked and left strewn on the ground. I had collected as many as I could and put them in water to take up the hill the next day.

The daffodils in the garden up there were always a picture, and we would pick those storm damaged with the spring wind and rain. I had laid out my clothes the night before and as I was getting ready our near neighbour, Eileen Kemish, appeared at the conservatory doorway which led outside.

My father had died early that morning and my mother had found him when she went in to take him a first cup of morning tea. It was Good Friday.

It was the beginning and entering of the seven years that were to lie between his death and my mother's.

6. The Hill of Difficulty, Miss Swannie & 'Goodbye' To My Father

The steep descent down the hill crossed Fernbrook Road and lower houses, and down a little footpath, led to the main street. The Pant-Yr-Avon was just a short arcade and next to the hairdresser, a door lead up the staircase, blue carpeted, to the small apartment above where for the autumn and spring before my father died I had lived.

The gable of the front window of the hillside home, I could just see as the leaves thinned in the autumn weeks and the garden I missed with a yearning too great after I returned down the bottom of the hill (the summer had contained deep and wounding unhappiness. I had taken this little apartment the year before, but stayed mostly up the hillside to meet my mother's wish until I was less unwell. It was a wish of duty).

I grieved in a way which was uncontainable and failed to get the strength I needed to again leave Wales. To go down to the Chalice Well was my wish in vain, somewhere there to live.

STATEMENT OF CASE: ROSEBAY WILLOW HERB

The writings of Wellesley Tudor Pole had given me this wish to know the Chalice Well Garden at Glastonbury, *A Man Seen Afar* with Rosamund Lehmann, and *The Writing On The Ground*. Presently my intense need to make this leaving, again from the sorrow of being in this land was quelled in the certainty that I need not go there, for my Chalice Well was instead to be made here. The many tributaries which flowed down through the hillside garden from the rising spring high above would seep through the rockery after rainfall. And I knew that was where my Chalice Well was to be. And I looked up the hillside, fervently realising it.

Verdant pastures... It was these that I craved. Only up the mountain through the fields, behind the convent, where the row of beech trees grew and the stream trickled over some small stones part of the way down, was there verdure. It was Pilgrim's Land, where Mr Greatheart and Christian had walked. But set where steepness was unyielding and severe and ungentle. It was the Hill of Difficulty.

Of difficulty... Only the harrowing years had testimony to tell of how much difficulty and of what design. What was it that was meaningful about this hillside home? It was nothing more than purpose built, centrally heated, and with no hearth fire, central to the very meaning of HOME. The mountain of grey granite on one side, the steep mountain lane with fields on either side of the other filled with spring lambs. And the lane between along past the waterfall, narrow then with tributaries of the spring that rose high above in the stone circle, trickling down the wall of Moel Lys below the overgrown rhododendrons of the disused driveway to only the fields beyond.

Unyielding, steep, and severe, the garden had nevertheless been made where the builders' earth had been left full of stones, and one large stone in the middle my father had to heave with a crowbar out of the way to make the lawn. Set to the side by the top of the garden, on steps that he put in were planted the wild strawberries my mother had brought with them from one small plant I had given her years before, and in the rest of the garden flowers bulbs and apple trees. Our honeysuckle too had been planted at the fence, and flowering currant, blackcurrant bushes and loganberry cane.

The large garden above, banked by trees, let through the rays of the first morning sun that filled the sunny kitchen all day and in which we listened to the words and music of morning meditation by Frank

Topping, in those years of unrewarded struggle. My father's illness ended all chance of pleasant years. My loss of life's belongs and meaning meant my only home was here, where I had come desolate on my journey and without strength in my own illness. What was it that was meaningful? It was a meaning, home before had not had of this kind indefinable and known only in some inner hidden way.

This land was not chosen, nor visited by either wish or will of mine. So what was the hidden meaning here? From this in the very beginning was I to become bonded in an ungentle, challenging land in contrast completely to the rural way I had in childhood years lived and yearned for again.

Living in rooms further down the hillside I missed this meaning and in intensely unhappy mourning, lived on here and then so many months there until I had returned to England to the small village near Evesham, where I spent nearly four more years. Only because my mother and father had long repined to return where they had known friends, and my aunt and uncle lived had I come back to North Wales on a goodbye visit. They wished to see my brother on his return visits to England from travelling expeditions. They went to stay in his house and changed their minds, only to return unable to make this decision that meant such upheaval to go back there.

My years in and around Evesham had been as unsheltered as previously. I had returned here unhappily, unwillingly, unable ever to feel it was a homeland to me. And it was on this return that I took Dilys' rooms above the salon.

What was it again that was special about this hillside home? From the three and a half years that I had spent in Sedgeberrow near Evesham and other surrounding villages, befriended so gratefully by Sian Emrys and her family, I had learnt the meaning of ley lines, life-lines through the earth. I had also learnt that some of these ley lines needed regeneration, so that a healing network could criss-cross this earth. Was it that a ley line needing this regeneration, ran down the hillside beneath this home? Walking up the stairs from the front door I came to have this certain feeling. As I reached the landing leading into the dining front room and living room, and kitchen, something pervaded the home that was indefinable then, but I was to realise, lay in the words of Sir Victor Goddard's foreword to the Life Story of Muriel Dowding. In the railway trucks in the siding of the station

STATEMENT OF CASE: ROSEBAY WILLOW HERB

below lay the mounds of granite quarried from mountain with names of the countries all over the world. Walking down the hillside one day with my mother after I first came here to visit my father in the sanatorium, there came to mind, then those words of invocation in Lord Dowding's book, *The Dark Star*, and I thought of them from then on during the years that were to follow: 'And now call on the Love Ray, And send it Out over this sad dark star...'

In this grey granite rock there were glistening specks of quartz that could spread light paths through the world, everywhere that it was used for road building purposes, just as it would 'light up' if x-ray beams were shone upon it in a glass case in a museum.

There had to be a meaning in my having found myself not merely here on a visit, but having to live here for years and years to come. On one of my birthdays, when my mother and my father had always remembered the birth that nearly lost us both her and I, my mother gave me a birthday card with some lines written called 'The Rose in the Wall'. This was the middle name she had given me... And as the rose creeps through the wall and the crannies, she gradually finds the light on the other side.

Whilst the grey and cadaverous side of the mountain was severe, the mountain lane was different. Turning to the left at the waterfall above the little green and along the narrow road, there it then rose steeply up to the right and past the houses (in so much more a benign setting), where the hedges were lined with blackberries. Winding on and up again the steep curve rounded Bryn Yolin, Miss Swannie's cottage, where we sat on more than one visit in front of her lovely log fire looking at so different a view. Then the hill rose further, to the final steep ascent up to the Pillars, which set bare above the tree-lined slope, heralded the Jubilee Pass.

Were you to leave the lane and walk across the fields past the white farmhouse, towards the far side of the mountain again, you would come to the steam down through the meadow and the line of beeches and elm, and through the gate, come down the other side past the reservoir and the (once) sheep track, where donkey cart travel was the only transport before the tarmac was laid by the water board.

This footpath had a wicket gate in it which led into the driveway that wound down parallel to it. The once private residence here was Craig Lwyd Hall. When the family no longer lived in it (by whom it was built, the Derbyshires, owners of the quarry at one time), it was used for German prison officers during the war, and then for convalescence when chalets were built in the grounds. In the course of time and in the change of further use, the caravans were placed there which made it into the present summertime enterprise for holiday visitors. The Hall itself stood grey and gaunt. Its view was across the seaward stretch to the island where the puffins and fulmars habited, at each end a lighthouse, which stood as two beacons, watched in times of illness from the bedroom window of the hillside house. I little knew I should ever spend my six years of endurance up there one day when the time came that I was to lose both my father and then my mother. The bonding with this home was the only meaning I had for being there and those bonds were indissoluble.

* * *

I had moved back down to my apartment above Dilys's salon on the Pant-Yr-Avon in September 1984. At the ending of this summer I felt incredibly ill, much, much more than before.

Christmas drew near, and I had spent many nights kneeling with my head in the armchair. 'Where streams of living water flow, my ransomed soul He leadeth.'. My ransomed soul... What was the meaning of it? A few days before Christmas itself, there was a knock on my landing door. At the top of the staircase there stood my two parents, my father and my mother. They wanted me to spend Christmas with them again, home up the hillside and my room, familiar was enfolding as was the rest of it.

In the New Year I returned until my birthday. Then when the first snow drops had appeared and were nodding the heads in the wind and sunshine, I went up again as they wished. Easter, following my mother's birthday, brought one of the turns of mind and temperament in my mother. It had grated upon my father and I realised one of those disparate intervals had again, as so frequently they did, transpired. Heartbreakingly understandable when the truth became known. But not until the very end for her, more than seven years after he had died. These times were lived with for years and years, and with the lonely forbearance with which he tolerated them but which I was unable to. For me it entailed hurt and desperation I could not bear. My heart could not contain it. Wounding incentive would only temporarily turn into kinder frame of mind, but then genuinely and with every concern.

Easter was the time of precious redemption, full of meaning for me. The daffodils that they had planted crowned this time of the year, and the garden was filled with forsythia and blossom from the two apple trees they had planted. The silver birch in the garden above and the cherry blossom also planted there was in blossom.

In my kitchen down at the bottom of the hill I kept two of my prayers on the lintel shelf which ran along the corner wall by the cooker. But, my mirror which I kept there also, had fragmented one winter night, frighteningly, as I stood it on the cooker to brush my hair. For no reason whatsoever, it suddenly lay in shattered pieces on the floor. There had been not even a tremor from the quarry. Nothing else had moved or even quivered. I trembled from head to foot, and knew I must wrap up the pieces. I did not know why this had happened. With a sense of unaccountable terror, I wrapped them in a cotton apron.

Spring turned into May and then Dilys made her announcement. There were visitors coming during the summer who always stayed in my particular apartment. Their granny always looked forward to it. She asked if I would move downstairs into the rooms renovated by Uncle Sam. Aunty Ivy and Uncle Sam stayed there whenever any decorating was being done in their bungalow, as Aunty Ivy could not breathe the smell of paint. This I therefore had to do at the end of that month.

There was little light in the rooms below until the middle of the afternoon, but there was a lilac tree just by the pathway that ran along the back there, and the steep garden led down into a clearing and then across a footbridge into the Dingle. This became my final refuge. Of all the years making home, looking for home, never finding home, this, together with my home up on the hillside, was the final resting place I reconciled myself to.

I nevertheless spent the next three months feeling very ill indeed down there and only towards the end of the summer did I manage to sort out my things.

I spent the oncoming winter in my dressing gown, going out with my clothes and coat over my night-things to either the grocery shop next door or the chemist or post opposite. My birthday was spent at home again for just the day. My heart went down when I reached the door, however. I did not know it. It was to be the final birthday on which I should ever receive their card. My father did not rise from his chair, but looked at me from troubled and unhappy eyes. They were as I had never seen them before, slightly bloodshot and clearly the result of another inharmonious interlude.

So concerned and unhappy was I myself that the very next day I went up to see them again. This time, he seemed better. He put on some gramophone records and when it came time to go to bed, he put on his coat to drive back down the hill. I left with a heavy heart.

My parents were preparing for a visit my aunt and uncle in the coming fortnight, and clearly there was no wish for me to be installed with them at the time of their visit. They needed my bedroom. My aunt had had an operation, and my mother wished her to come for a few days convalescence. I would not be needed during that time. The role of being a dependant daughter was one I did not wish to resume. Until there was a need, I would not return again.

There were two weeks to Easter and I prepared for this. On Maundy Thursday, I went down to sit by the stream through the trees in the Dingle for a breath of spring air, and was dismayed to see the daffodils lying everywhere, completely stripped and thrown down. I gathered them up and took them back to stand in water. Later that evening I laid my clothes ready to get dressed on Good Friday morning. It was to be my third day dressed that year. Still in my dressing gown the next morning, I suddenly saw my mother's close neighbour Eileen at the door. She said, "I have come to tell you your father died very early this morning."

Without an instant's hesitation I suddenly thought of the blackbird I had released from the conservatory not long before that had flown in by mistake, seemingly chased by a robin. Holding him in a yellow duster in my hand and going to the open doorway, I released him. And he flew straight like a dart down between the trees.

I could not rush up to the home upon the news. I had to sit and gather the reserves I knew I had to find. Dilys came down and told me if I wished, she would give me a lift at midday. I did not want to send for any other kind of lift. I could not walk up the hill. I reached the home to find my mother's neighbour Eileen with her, waiting until I had arrived before she went. My father had been ill with pneumonia for two days before, and I had never been told. She herself had gone to keep her appointment with Dr O'Burn at the hospital, which I had not known she had. It was for the fibromyalgic pain under her left shoulder, for which she was constantly prescribed Brufen tablets. She had left the key in the door, and a note to let himself in. I could not believe it! It increased with immense and devastating hurt the grief of bereavement. He was no longer in my room, but already in the chapel of rest. They had taken him at half-past ten. I had my arms full of daffodils. I put some at the foot of my bed which he had been lying in.

We chose Mozart's *Ave Verum* to be played for his service, and Donald Roberts asked us what we would like to do with the arrangement of flowers for his coffin, and whether we would like to contribute them to the Heart and Stroke Association. I would have like to have had them in the house for the next week. My mother felt it would be alright however, for them to go to the hospital. They have so many flowers there. Surely they would have been superfluous. When asked if she would like to see him in the chapel and to think about it, she later said, "I think I'd like to just say goodbye to Dad."

I wanted her to go alone. Having not said my goodbye to him in the house, I could not bear to. She returned peacefully, with the calmest look on her face, and said, "He looked so rested as he lay." It was Saturday, Easter Eve. On Sunday morning Mr Roberts called to collect me. He opened up the door of what seemed no more than a little hut lying under the massive granite of the quarry where we had sometimes ventured at blackberrying time, when the berries had all been picked elsewhere. I, too, was instilled with the peace my mother had. And more than peace, peace passing understanding. He looked radiant somehow. Beautiful. With a beauty I had not seen on his earthly face. But which had transfigured him, momentarily once, when he had come out of hospital and was suffering all the vexatiousness of his illness, and the nausea that streptomycin had left him with.

As I stroked his lovely hands, his engineers working hands, so skilled with tools, I looked at his lovely long fingers, thinking of his longing himself to play the piano. Though I had loved my piano all those years, he played it only for a little while when it first came to us from my grandmother and grandfather when they moved. I learnt by ear the pieces he played from a tattered, thin little music book with a brown paper cover. *Increasing Pleasure.* I had the gift from him, of my love of music. And I did not want to leave him. I would have kept some vigil, if I had a little private chapel in my own home. Suddenly that meant so much to me. A private place of prayer and contemplation. So reluctantly did I look my last upon him. So well did I than understand the meaning of the words, 'made perfect by the love of Our Lord Jesus Christ.'

On going home I realised that concept I had held for them was so true. Gems we are… in the making. It is the raw materials of this life that undergo that divine alchemy. Only our worthiness can be the alchemical gold.

My dad, I knew, was worthy.

No memories of cherished nearness did I have to give me this. For of heart and mind I had come from a different sphere. There had never been the moment to moment lovingness there that by temperament was my need. I had never had this nourishment. The sense of loneliness, lostness it seemed in him, was in the way. And I was to learn in times still to come of my own pain, why.

Not for me, the words of Kathleen Tynan of her father, in one of the very many poems she had written, blessed with such kind heaven. I had never sat on Father's knee with a story, nor run to him with my tears. The deepest affection I knew he had for me, as I knew from that time in the sanatorium when he had called for me in delirium. But in our ordinary days and life he had been lost from me. Worse than lost, was in the communication that meant so much misunderstanding had been buried deeply in him during the years. I had been hurt for it, and deeply wounded. Now, and from the time of my mother's death, consummately, this was to be comforted. But the terrible price was to come for it all.

Everything that I made I use to bring to you.
Was it a song, why, then, 'twas a song to sing for you.
Was it a story, to you I was telling my story.
Ah, my dear, could you hear 'mid the bliss and glory?
Did anyone praise me, to you I said it all over.

My laughter for you: how we laughed in the days past recover!
My tears and my trouble were for you: did anyone grieve me
I carried it straight to the love that was sure to relieve me.

It took seven and a half more years for the deterioration that was to come in my mother to bring her release. And to know that nothing misconstrued could be any longer. Nothing mendacious could have meaning. Only the transparent truth would be there for them. With this I could live.

But never the grief.

I went up the garden steps on coming back from the chapel of rest, to spend a while up there. The sun was glistening on the still snow-capped mountain, through an April rain. The elements together for him.

7. 'Goodbye' To My Mother, 'The Soul's Dark Cottage'

My mother's uncertainty and confusion in many ways was troubling. Wanting to pay the bills just as my father always had done, she asked me to help. "Where do I sign my name?" She would ask, when opening her pension book. "Will you be going down the hill today? If so, could you get something for lunch?" I would meet her coming up the hill, having forgotten completely the errand. I would collect two night dresses from my rooms and any needs to take back with me.

On one occasion I sat to have a rest in the chair for a few minutes. Presently Dilys' voice called down. "Lisabeth, your mother has shut herself out, and Margaret Watts has rung up to ask if you can go back with your key. She is round with her."

I picked the carrier up I had laid down on the bed and switched off the electric blanket I had put on for a few minutes to give it an airing. There were droplets of water covering it. I felt with my hand along the bed. To my incredulity, the sheets were soaked when I felt them. I knew it was damp down there. Dilys knew. But when describing how difficult it was for Uncle Sam to make the all the paper stick to the wall, she explained how he had solved it in one place, by fitting a 'drinks cupboard'. Another part of the wallpaper I wiped down regularly and I had told her. I knew I should have things attended to however. I discovered I had been paying too much for my heating, from the electricity reading, when I went through my mother's bills - an extra half penny per unit. During the course of the winter I had spent down there that came to nearly seventy pounds.

I went down on the morning the environmental officer was meant to call. By half-past eleven he still had not come, and I had promised to go and have a morning cup of tea with the couple staying next to me, in similar refurbished rooms, whose little girl had just had her third birthday. No sooner had I sat down with the welcome tea, than Dilys' voice called out! She had been in the garden burning some cuttings, the salon being closed on a Monday. "A gentleman had called to see you."

The gentleman had gone, and on the mat of the open doorway, just ajar, was his card. Mr Sutcliffe, environmental health officer. He must have spoken to her. Nothing more was said.

I rang up and said to him the mildew and green verdigris I had discovered in my things needed attending to. He replied that, 'It was between myself and the owner.' I answered him that it was his job, as my rent was being paid by the council, to tell the owner they should not be allowed to let the rooms in such a state. It was completely in vain.

It was not until the following year that I learnt that Councillor Tom Clarke had, previous to their request I move into those rooms, and previous presumably to their renovation, placed a dereliction order down there.

In the meantime I had a notice duly served on me by Dilys, to move from their private rooms by Friday at 6 p.m. And, "We will read the meter for the electricity together," she had written. I was in no way able to have any confrontation with Dilys. My nerves were on the edge of disintegrated resilience. My mother would not have a window open. Not any window. She insisted on having the heating on. Our boiler smelled. It had always smelled. I had it serviced. It made no difference - it definitely smelled, and the oily smell sickened me. Even the toilet window was kept closed and on my trying by all reason to have it open, my mother hit me. For the first time in my life, this had completely unnerved me. It was followed by some kind of struggle over the garden rake a few days on. In the garage was our electricity meter. She became obsessed with switches (the boiler switch being switched off and on for no reason other than she fiddled with it. It made the smell nine times worse).

Then we would have a completely harmonious interval. She would come looking for me in case there was anything she had done. Was there anything wrong? Was I alright? I was looking tired to her. Would I have a rest, a cup of tea, anything else she could make me? I did not know whether I was more confused or touched by these times. I remember similar concerns before when my father was alive and he and I would be at a loss to answer her. Two eyes that were liquid question marks would look at you and you would have just no idea what to say. No recollection had she of the invective that had made him quiet or me. If one tried to say in reply what was wrong it made things worse.

I watched a programme called The Healing Arts. Somehow, I knew the replenishment of my dwindling reserves must be through this, for a wing and a prayer were no longer sufficient. The ways I had transcended the years were not possible now. My mother would take her Brufen tablets twice over, and her back pain would be intermittent. She would have days that were completely disparate and it could not go on. She would get worse in her confusion, running backwards and forwards in her nightie with a Dettol bottle in her hand to do something for the pain. The doctor prescribed the tablets like dolly-mixtures. Then I would have to ring a neighbour to give me some help because she was on the floor and I could not, by myself, get her in the bed. There were no longer two pairs of hands without my father.

She had to be hospitalised for having too many of these, but they were just dished out the same. I could not believe the doctor's denial of help or concern. "Your mother is perfectly capable of being independent," she retaliated, "and so are you," I was making a fuss!

I did not think it was a fuss to be worried about my mother breaking her femur bone again. That had been a trial. Those words burned into my mind as the time went on, and as the years went on.

STATEMENT OF CASE: ROSEBAY WILLOW HERB

Those words were to be the legacy which she, as home-doctor for fourteen years, was to leave me.

Her retirement was in the pleasant uplands of Llanfairfechan. My road was to be the breaking of mind and resilience.

* * *

I did not know what to do with the notice I had been confronted with by Dilys. I turned to the furniture showroom which was formerly the Co-operative. The present owners lived with their sheepdog up Mountain Lane, and we had met on walks. I was indebted to them for their kind reception to my dilemma. They duly had my things collected by their removal van at midday on the Friday and with a heavy heart I left a note with the keys for Dilys to find.

This had become a final refuge to end the harrowing years of looking for home. Home I realised I would never find with the hearthfire I needed. I had come to reconcile that home, always remaining in the place of my heart, and this departure was as harrowing as any I had made. I had little sleep, packing in the few hours she had given me. No altercation could I have with her now.

Six weeks later I had to make other arrangements for my things I knew. For kind as the couple had been to me in looking after my things in this time, they were, in fact, moving down to Shropshire. They had spent three years in North Wales and decided not to stay. There was nowhere else to find.

* * *

I went up the mountain, as I had done years before, to where I stayed among the chalets and caravans let in the summertime, and was told the rent now would be too dear for me to afford. But they had part of the hall to spare. I went up to look at the large sitting room, entered through a door at the very end of the landing, and bedroom. These I would have to take, I had said, if I could find nowhere else in the six weeks available. For somewhere to keep my things.

I never ever imagined I should live up there. It was some temporary place which was merely part of the passing trauma of time and circumstance and the bereavement which I was not able to even to feel. So were the days demanding in other ways.

I was, in the end, fifteen months on, to return up there from hospital to spend the endurance of 6 more years challenging every last weakened strength I was able to gather.

It was the last leave taking I could ever make. This, I said, was the last time it would ever happen to me. The very last. Ever.

8. Into The Dark

It was a year later that I went to see Dr Tony Dickinson. By August the head of Social Services, Lucille Hughes had been told how I was being treated locally. Having gone down to the chemist I had met Mrs Marjorie Hughes, retired from the library. Walking back up the hill with me she said she was going to a meeting that evening and would speak with Tom Clarke, longstanding councillor and closely involved with the Social Services. He telephoned me the next day and told me he was visiting Lucille Hughes. The only retort I had had in my distress, from them, had been that "Families are cruel to one another... that is a fact of life." And the rest had been in that vein. Lucille Hughes was told. She instructed Tom Clarke to take me for an interview with the head of the Social Services locally.

Joan Clarke drove us in. We were told that my treatment had been unsympathetic. Someone else would be sent. A few days later notification arrived there was to be a visit again from the same woman. I rang Tom Clarke. In every exasperation he said, as I myself felt, it had been an utter waste of time. But he was not for going back to them to say so. "Tell them where to go, Lisabeth," he said. "Just tell them where to go."

With nothing but this desolation left, there was nothing to do but to try to find the replenishment I needed in some way to enable myself to cope. But to travel to Chester now and back in one day was more than I had strength for, and I dearly needed somewhere to stay for some respite and care; Would Dr Dickinson's receptionist know anywhere restful I could stay? I asked her.

In the end I made the journey, to return spent entirely. Dr Dickinson had waived his fee and told me I needed the consultant Dr Ronald Finn at Liverpool Royal Infirmary. With every understanding, he said he would not want to go to Liverpool either. I said that once upon a time it would have been a day's outing to have come to Chester that day, now it had meant taking my courage in both hands to step on a train. I had, he said, the Myalgic Viral Disease needing recognition and research, and its beginnings were in my early childhood.

I had described my childhood illnesses, scarlet fever, whooping cough, following which I had whooped for the next two winters, the measles and the mumps, the chicken pox. And he then asked if I had ever had stomach trouble. Our very first holiday away in Devon had been marred by this. In fact it was then that I became so completely and weakeningly exhausted, tired with each day spent picnicking on the sand dunes, where I would lay my head down on the coats and go to sleep, to wake just as wearingly tired. This was no holiday for me. I missed my fields and the lane, the hay-making and blackberry time. I was stricken one morning at the breakfast table with excruciating stomach pain and back upstairs, lay with this all day, sleeping and waking with the same waves of sick pain. The doctor was called in and said if I was no better that evening to call him again. By tea-time, I was brought up some lemon-meringue pie. I had not ever eaten anything so pacifying and emollient as in that hour, and I gratefully ate a second helping, after which the good-natured woman who was looking after us said there was still a small piece left in the dish, 'Would I like it!'

I told Dr Dickinson all this and suddenly he stopped writing and put his pen down. "Does light hurt your eyes?" he said. I had found the intense glare of sun on sand too much to bear and said so. But besides this, there was the pain in my ears at any loud noise that I couldn't bear. The next summer had been the RAF Jubilee at Farnborough and my uncle had tickets for us. All afternoon, I lay in the back of the car with coats over my head to drown out the sound of roaring aircraft and later was told by my mother my uncle had been hurt that I had not enjoyed the so special occasion, with the Red Arrows flying in formation and other memorable aircraft on display. This distressed me more, and I had no idea how to contend with both my tiredness and various forms of misery, and then criticism as well. Besides this, though I travelled without being carsick, the smell of petrol affected me whenever we went into the petrol station as soon as my father lit a cigarette. Moderated as a smoker he usually rolled his own but the combination of smoke and petrol sank to my stomach and made the next few miles sickly. Fat cooking affected me in the same way and I could not stand the smell of bacon, one of the early recollections I carry to this day. For me, it is as appalling as cooked chicken.

I received every sympathy for these things and was told by Dr Dickinson they were part of the environmental sensitivities characterising why I was by then so unwell. He followed this by saying there wasn't any honest way he could help me and that he felt insistently Dr Finn should. My disconsolation left me with two hours to spend until getting the return train and with nowhere else, I sought a corner of the cathedral gardens and there shed my tears of grief. But how many more were to come.

* * *

Beyond these first ten years, Dr Dickinson hadn't continued. To have taken money from me for treatment, he said, would be dishonest of him. "But I am still here," he had said. "I am not pushing you from pillar to post." Dr Finn's confirmation would help me more. The remaining medical case had to be given to him, of a year's physiotherapy, and remaining pain in my back, neuralgia which I had not had before, but which became constant, together with the cold, in my legs. And then the sleeping through each afternoon, which started after the polio vaccine. Unable to keep awake through these hours, I would sleep with my head on the desk. And after five o'clock at home, the only thing I wanted was peaceful evening time. My piano was my indispensable consolation. I had been devoted to children's nursing up until that time. Then I started to play for children's ballet, which eventually became a strain that increased upon me, until I was looking at a maze of black and white notes, and my memory wouldn't serve me any longer for the long hours I sat, my back aching, playing through each of the classes, including Greek dance which I loved. Its lovely spacious movements were a dance style that flowed naturally and after a presentation at a final summer garden party, nearly five years of classes came to an end.

This had been very much from the trauma of leaving the very unhappy grammar school to which I had to change, and from which I would have returned to my very good secondary school, had I not felt it to be a retrograde thing to do. I regretted it for the rest of my life. But none of it, I knew would have changed the course of my undermined wellbeing. There was no description to give to how ill I was. I did not think of it as being a disease of my immune system. All these years were to have to pass until it was given a name. It was weeks before I would see Dr Finn, and so in cold October I went to stay at the Retreat House in Abbey Square in Chester before the second half of my journey.

* * *

There was a tea-kettle on the landing, and I was given a jug of milk to make myself tea early the next morning. But having walked the distance to the coach station I was near collapse when I reached it. Dr Finn's receptionist told me to wait, and I did so until twenty five past eleven. My consultation was meant to be from eleven until twelve. He asked me why I had come.

Lost for words, I recounted my reasons for going to Dr Dickenson and that it was at his behest. "He said it would be dishonest of him to treat me," I said, "and take my money privately." I thought the background of my visit to Dr Finn would be known to him. With this, he concurred, but then informed me it would be necessary to go into his hospital ward. It would be negligent of him not to have me under his observation, and he would only write to my home doctor under these circumstances. With that, he put his arm on my shoulder and showed me out.

STATEMENT OF CASE: ROSEBAY WILLOW HERB

* * *

Back in Abbey Square I spent my recovery night more desolate than I knew how to bear. To make this journey a second time would be impossible. I moved to a guest house nearly a mile out of Chester. Nearby there was a surgery, and I was taken there to a very kind Dr Hughes. In every contrast to my home surgery I was listened to very sympathetically, and a few days later received a copy of a letter, written to the Social Services in Chester, confirming that I waited for a bed in Dr Finn's ward for diagnosis, and needed somewhere during my last weeks of waiting, to lay my head. For to have remained indefinitely, was not possible. Bookings meant that my room in a fortnight's time was needed. By then, I was drained with every further direction I had turned in to find somewhere to stay. I did not want to go back into the city. Finally, I was taken in by the Refuge for Battered Women in a house at the end of Vicarage Road, and realised I could not wait on for Dr Finn's vacancy. My visit had been in vain. Together with Tony Dickinson, I had no heart to get back to him. I was utterly, heartbreakingly, demoralised.

On the train journey back, I thought of my bedroom, and that iridescent blue light that had filled it the morning I had departed. I had not wanted to leave. Nor should I have done, I realised now. But how was I to go on with my mother? Needful of me, by turns, and disparate the next, the inconsistency, and the injuries I had sustained, had brought me down to no further resilience. With this I could not go on. There was no return possible, home.

* * *

The few days I had spent, weeks earlier, sorting out the possessions which had been moved up the mountain, had tired me more than I could deal with. I had sat on the grass before leaving to go back down the hillside, watching a bee on the rhododendron bush through a haze of tiredness as intense as I was going to know for the next six years.

Depleted and more tired than tired, I could barely live in these rooms, large and yet unbreathable in some way. The long casement windows I had to have open failed to refresh the air. Only the night brought a clearing sense of mountain breath. On Sunday morning I sat at the open casement, when a car drew up at the top of the bank. It was Paul Hillman, who looked after the garden at the large convent. He had been to my home, and I was not there. I told him, I had been back only since Friday, and that a letter had come from the hospital on Saturday morning notifying me to arrive at Ward 22, Sefton Hospital on Monday.

I had telephoned, I said to Paul, and told the sister on the Ward it was quite impossible for me to make the journey again. She had clucked and fussed, saying Dr Finn had wanted me in, and if I got on the train again, she said, people would help. Paul said he would come for me on Monday at lunchtime. I knew it was impossible to go back home without some upholding toward the turns of heart, mind, and temperament of my mother. I could not cope any longer with the leaking oil boiler, nor could I stand its vibrating. And my mother had taken to refusing to have any of the windows open. The nearby district nurse tried to speak to Doctor Hutt, but to no good. She had already denied her help. My mother's confusions meant she would go down the hill without purse or money and would come home with her back pain again. Deliveries of groceries and fish were turned away. Paul came up on Monday. I knew the only thing was to go.

I could not leave before half past twelve and as the train slowly pulled away from the platform I felt the rock face of the mountain look on as its nearness receded, and the train went into the tunnel through which it would travel on to Conwy. Mounds of excavated earth were heaped by the side of the embankment as the first stages of the A55 were begun, years of petitioning having been laid eventually aside. Further devastation to Mother Earth, with her many sick children.

Never could such nightmare be imagined to come. The final stage was by bus from Liverpool station, to my bewilderment, to a hospital another half hour's journey with only standing room in the home-going hour of crowds in the dark dreariness of November rain. Finally put down by the driver from a nearly empty bus, all the other passengers having disembarked, I was left in the middle of nowhere, with only a long driveway indicated to me across the road, with distant lights dimly in a line.

I managed to get to the middle island of the road as oncoming lights speeded both ways towards me and then eventually the rest of the way across. A few yards on I sank down onto the kerb of the driveway which stretched ahead. Presently, more headlights started to come towards me and eventually to pass on. What dark kind of figure I must have been I do not know. More frightened with every step, I did not know whether walk or crawl, or whether I was noticed, or how to go on. There was some small doorway in sight, lit up, and eventually I reached it to find myself standing in an empty corridor with miles of linoleum stretching out of sight. I heard the sound of a trolley being trundled along but it went away. Presently I heard it again and this time called out and a stooping figure appeared. He did not seem to have the ability of speech, but he turned and went and then reappeared with a wheelchair which he must have been pushing. This ricketed along for some time and then he stopped by a doorway, went in, and came back again, and then disappeared. A few seconds later the door opened and a figure who would have to be called a nurse stared at me. Then another came and just looked. Then a voice said, "Who's that woman in the doorway?"

After some delay another uniformed nurse came and demanded to know what I was doing there. In tears of exhaustion and pain I simply held on to the letter in my hand which I had shown the porter with Ward 22 on it, Sefton Hospital. "Well, where have been?" was the reply. "Dr Finn has been looking for you all day."

I said, "I have been making this journey."

* * *

I was pushed to a bed, told to take my clothes off and get into it. I was cold and shivering and the lights were brilliant to have to endure. The sister came to the bed and said, "Dr Finn had been over four times from the Infirmary to see if I had arrived for him." A colleague of his would come over now, she explained. Dr Finn never saw me for another 48 hours and never knew how I had arrived. After I had told him in his consulting room what a journey the travelling had been for me that day, he'd simply patted me condescendingly. Now a nurse came up with some weighing scales which she proceeded to let drop with full weight on the floor. I was told to get out of bed and stand on them and she then sat down with notepad in hand and asked for some information. I told her I thought Dr Finn's notes would be on hand as I had gone through my case history with him.

"No," she said, "this is for nursing notes."

I did not know how to talk. But she asked, when the pains I had now in my legs first began. I said, "When I was seven and eight years old. I was told they were 'Growing pains.'"

The second nurse passed the bed and heard me. "Ooh, I have got those pains as well, she said. Now they're *withering pains*."

After a Dr Staffer had arrived and I had gone through the same thing again, the first nurse came back and said, "I saved a dinner for you, do you want it?"

When she brought it I told her, I was sorry, I did not. She then said something to an auxiliary nurse who came up to the bedside, and utterly too drained to make word or sound to her, I just broke down. "Oh, alright then, she replied, "if you don't want to talk." Her implied tone was that I was uncooperative and refused. I could no longer believe there was reality in where I was, nor the pain I was in. Nor the cold. The only thing to do was… to try and put my clothes on in bed. The sister then came up with a fleece for my legs and presently another. And between these two I tried to keep warm for the next four days.

The lights had been intolerable and did not go out, so eventually a lady in the bed opposite got up and turned them off. Wanting to go to the toilet, she was the only help and kindly looked after me for those four days. It was her leaving on the eve of my fourth night that made me know I could not remain any longer. The sister had told me I was in that ward because it was where Dr Finn had two spare beds, and there was a side ward in which there was a very ill young boy. His ward in the Infirmary was full and he was very anxious to have me in. A second colleague of his had been to me the next morning and told me he had to test me for 200 possible allergens, and if none of them were making me ill, then Dr Finn's confirming diagnosis would be Myalgic Encephalomyelitis. My head was so painful with lights that I had a headache to end all headaches, of migraine intensity, and the sister had turned them off that morning. He wanted them back on. He needed to see, he had said. Like Dr Hutt.

It was the next morning that Dr Finn came. He looked at the results of the many needles I had had up and down my arm. I was allergic only to mushrooms and chicken. I loved mushrooms, but they made me ill so I could never have them, and, "I never eat hens," I told him.

"Well, my dear, I think you need a good rest now," he said. I told him I knew I needed a rest. Nevermore had I needed a rest, but nobody had understood that, least of all Dr Ann Hutt. Nervous debility had been her definition, for years, and no comprehension was there of what nervous debility needed in the way of help. Not the suffering of bright lights for one thing.

In the event of my mother taking too many of her Brufen tablets, she had eventually been called one night by her neighbour, whom I had to get round in order to help me get my mother off the floor. Bending over the bed, the bedroom lamp on, she had then said she needed the top light. The ambulance men whom she called to take her in to Llandudno hospital were the only ones with a sympathetic word, when they switched the light out for me, and told me to make myself a bedtime drink. "Look after yourself," they said.

With similar kindness the lady in the ward bed opposite looked after me, until the eve her husband came for her, telling me her own illness had been a long time being diagnosed. She worked in the children's hospital and had been off work for a year until they discovered her kidneys were the cause of her illness. She had also been on Brufen tablets for arthritis. She had had them for ten years and her kidneys had shrivelled to the size of walnuts. Provided with a kind of catheter, she had gone home to wait until she could return for a transplant.

I told Dr Finn I was indeed, in need of a rest, but that lights and the televisions were too bright and too loud for me and there was no rest. With his coat over his arm he returned to my bedside after some while in the sister's office, and said. "Well, my dear, I want you to know that if you change your mind, you are welcome to stay," And explained that he would write to my home surgery of his diagnosis. There had been one red wheel at the top of my arm which he passed off as Candida yeast. "Everyone comes up like that," he said. I later wished I had thought that to say, that everyone has it. But not in its secondary and ill-making mycelia form. I had been refused medication by Dr Ann Hutt. He made no promise of instructions.

Because of my treatment by the social services, the welfare officer at the hospital made me a visit. If the social workers at home had been dismissive, he was the reverse. Despite the nightmare of the four days I had gone through it would have been worth it if his kindness and immense goodness had been followed up by them. However, they had ignored Dr Hughes in Chester and were to ignore the hospital as well, back in North Wales.

A new nurse who had been on duty was sent with me in the hospital car to the train, after an unsatisfactory EEG done by the sister on the ward had to be done again, and a rickety journey undergone over some cobbles in the cold wind to another part of the hospital. While waiting back in the ward, I picked up from the books lining the windowsill behind my bed one volume. It said, *Under My Coat*, by Edna O'Brien. Inside the frontispiece were the lines from a sonnet of William Shakespeare's.

Why didst thou promise such a beauteous day
And make me travel forth without my cloak.

As the nurse saw me into the train and the doors closed, she stood and held my hand at the window. "Hospital isn't the right place to be for you," she said. "You need stillness and quiet." The train slowly pulled away and she diminished into a small figure before eventually disappearing from sight as the train went into the tunnel. "I will remember you," she said. "You will be in my prayers."

* * *

The weeks to follow were a long and dark trial. Barely could I stand to make a piece of toast, my back was in so much pain. Trying to walk from the hospital car, the nurse had said to me, "You must have inflammation in the bone." Dr Finn's words were to try and read all I could about research. Sue Finley finally sent me a letter of sympathy, having formed with Martin Lev and Dr Anne MacIntyre the beginnings of the campaign into this research. I had gone to Dr Finn with one thought uppermost in my mind. *To go through with this* I thought, must *contribute to the discovery of some further medical knowledge*. From 1970 onwards I had never believed I would go into a hospital again willingly.

STATEMENT OF CASE: ROSEBAY WILLOW HERB

* * *

My strengths were spent out day after day and I had to endure the banging of heavy slammed doors, and the unventilated landing meant the residual smoke there made it impossible to breathe. I used my outside staircase from the balcony, its dilapidated wooden rail unsafe, and the steps limed with moss. One day, coming back from breathing a little green air, I reached the bottom of the staircase to make the climb back. I slipped on the second step, and fell on my side. My side that I had fallen on before, under the beech tree by the gate where the stile went over the stone wall, and that had been so painful since. I had no idea how to climb the rest of the steps. Back inside the casement window eventually, I lay on the carpet and wept. I lay as days and weeks went by with the large casement open despite the cold and thought of the land I had made this, years before. The land of Lothlórien. Where brave Frodo and his two companions, after they had travelled through Mordor, found rest, hospitality, and healing. And where they had received their three gifts from the Lady Galadriel when they departed. I thought of the garden down the hillside with burnt out longing. I thought of the home there. I thought of my room. I thought of the many mornings, so consecrated sometimes as the sun came through the trees and the words of meditation to which we listened on *Pause for Thought* on the wireless to the 'Lord of the Morning'.

I thought of the meadow where the footpath went along to the stream the other side of the stile. This is where Mr Greatheart had walked with Christian and the shepherd boy sang his song in Pilgrim's Progress. And I thought of Narnia, and of the wonderful lion Aslan, the children and their question when he left them a final time... "Where has Aslan gone to?" And the answer they were given.

"Didn't you know, he has other realms to look after besides ours."

It was Aslan's warm breath upon the icy frozen land that brought it to life and spring flowers opened, birds sang, and icicles melted into running streams and riverlets. This was Aslan's mountain, but it was, too, these other lands, pictured in music (for me) by the cascading Grieg's Piano Concerto. The ultimate tone poem. This place of endurance for me where I stayed was part of this. Having represented both war and peace, holding German prison-officers after the last war and being used for convalescence before being taken over for other purposes, I could only hold what concepts of good and of peace I may.

The beginning of January however held blackout for two days. Without warmth, without light, the darkest time of the year. When next I ventured to get a lift down the mountain, my driver Dai Evans, obtained a quarter-size gas cylinder for me, giving me a burner fitment for the top he had, to go with it. On the wireless I heard Joan Wilkinson, Gordon Wilkinson's wife talking about the loss of her daughter at Enniskillen. Asked how she felt whenever she walked past the war memorial where her husband and daughter lay under bombed rubble, she said, "Oh, I have to beautify that place!" Just as I had tried myself the previous summer, planting the rescued flowers from Saturday night vandalism in the flower pots Paul had given me, bringing some of my own in which to plant broken forsythia from which I had taken cuttings of geraniums and blue campanulas, and placing a bowl for a birdbath in the previous hot summer weather of the few days I had spent here sorting my things out.

I was moved by Joan Wilkinson's words: I would send her some flowers, some bulbs, they would flower every year. I would send these for her war memorial.

9. Many Lands

Craig Lwyd Hall stood gaunt on the mountainside. The long, winding driveway upwards had been flanked by willow poplars when I had stayed there in the first two years in North Wales, for the weeks of April and May.

Now they had all been pollarded. The Derbyshire family who had been builders of the place, owners of the quarry then, had long since departed. The chalets came to be there when it was used for convalescence at the end of the war, when the captured German prison officers were no longer held there.

It had then been used as a finishing school for young ladies, then a remand home for boys. So its use had constantly changed, from war to peace, from learning social graces to rehabilitating the present workers in the grounds in the world of useful work.

There was, however, to be no rehabilitation for me.

Hospital instructions from the welfare visitor to my bedside were ignored by the social services. I had a card pushed under my landing door one day asking if I needed any shopping from a certain Mrs

Griffiths. I returned the card telling my needs. There was no post box up the mountain however. In the course of time my letters were posted either by the milkman who came only three times a week, the postman himself who took them for me sometimes, or I had to telephone from the entrance hall for a local driver to collect me. My needs and necessities I could only get this way, going into Conwy or sometimes just the Fairy Glen shop and post office. I went no more into Penmaenmawr below. The card was never answered by Mrs Griffiths. Only the social worker of before called eight weeks later. The one who had been reported by Councillor Clarke for her uncompassionate treatment, and simply instructed to come again by the head of the social services after he had reprimanded her. Tom Clarke had told me in exasperation over the telephone, "Oh, tell them where to go Lisabeth... Just tell them where to go!"

I asked her why they had never sent anybody to meet the train when I returned from the consultant Dr Finn, and why it had taken eight weeks to come, and why no help was being given me now.

To this she replied, "We only help the sick and the elderly."

* * *

I saw this social-welfare visitor in eight week intervals when she would send a notice saying she intended to come. I would have to get up for her at usually about three o'clock in the afternoon for the same kind of inane interview, and when one week I had forgone this very necessary time of rest for nothing, having sat up tired for her, to answer the door until five-thirty. I told her there was little use in my continuing to receive her. I had to leave a warm bed where I had needed to remain. Nothing of the real suffering everyday with this illness registered with her. The intensely ill state I had now reached was infinitely worse than that before I had gone into hospital. In the same way, it failed to register downstairs.

Taking my rent into the office, it would be signed for, and sometimes, if Amanda Thornley was there, I would be nicely spoken to. David Thomas, the accountant was also pleasant enough to me. Even David Thornley, when he was there. The incivilities for the rest of the time, however, were more than I was able to endure.

I heard a talk given by Brian Blessed describing his acting days working in rep, and the daytime job he had labouring where he suffered so similarly, I knew exactly what he was describing, the meaning of what he said. He went for speech lessons regularly, riding on his bicycle the 15 miles to his teacher's house. Reviews of a particularly good performance had been in the press after a while, but in one of these, a critic had decided to say he had 'overstated his part.' The other workers where he was labouring in the daytime pinned it up on a tree. He was taunted for about six weeks by this and their calling out, until he was on his way again for his speech lesson with his dynamo on in the dusk. To the sound of this, the voices that had been taunting him all these weeks went through and through his head, until he arrived, finally, in a state of unconscious nervous collapse.

It had taken six weeks to bring him to this. It happened to me for six years. It had become the voice of a further social worker who had visited me, it had been doctors, it had been a Citizen's Advice Bureau worker who had insisted on my telling her the background to the legal help I had needed since taking the apartment in 1986. "Haven't you got family?" she had retorted, when I told her the matter. "I've been a nurse, tell me," when I mentioned the unhappiness with my mother. Finally, having indulged her with my confidences and the refusal of help from the home doctor for myself or for Her, I departed with her instructions to go back later that week when their visiting solicitor would be there on the Thursday morning. I had already been spent of my strength making this visit, but on Thursday morning I had duly returned.

She had prepared for my visit herself, laying out some legal reference books. She told me I could get Legal Aid, and to go and find a solicitor who would look into things for me. I replied this is what I had come back for, and that she had also intended to be of some help in mediation with the doctor regarding my mother. She would have none of this, and sent me back with the words, "Some of us must learn our mothers don't love us."

The Pat Corns social worker had said, "Families are cruel to one another, that is a fact of life." And later, the Nesscliffe woman. She had taken hours telling me she had transferred from the DSS to being a Social Worker, and had read some of the medical notes on my file, and that something must be looked into, following which she looked into nothing!

Upon remarking to her that she hadn't, she had then leaned forward, and with her face in front of me, had said, "Well, I have considered everything and I believe if you were sufficiently self-motivated, you would do something about these things yourself, don't you? There is a saying, 'God helps those who help themselves.'"

She had requested to make use of my bathroom, invading the privacy of my bedroom to do so, and this was her retort, for the courtesy. I wished I had sent her to the end of the landing. The toilets down there didn't work. There were cloakrooms downstairs. I could have told her she had passed them on the way. That I was not a public convenience. All this only went through my head later. And continued to do, as to this very day. For there was far worse to come.

There were further programmes as time went on, through which I learned there were others this happened to. The series was called 'Never the Same Again'. It was a well-chosen title. No leave-taking does such insult take of your mind which with the increasing repetition from those trained to invade the integrity with which we live the lives we have. It happens with the repetition that only counsellors, community mental health clinics (working with Mind and workshops distributing their transformative literature describing their therapies), and the endless stream of books all telling you of the need to change your thoughts, can inflict. They reinterpret the interviews we are gratuitously suffered to give. Nothing that is conveyed to them is undenigrated. We part with the privacy of thought and being we are made of, demeaned and undervalued. Every college syllabus now includes this, as well as every complimentary form of treatment. The forgone conclusion is in the negative, by these, and the writers they read. Their written reports follow.

No mediation have they in mind, which is constructive, and burning distress leads into ultimate torment. Nights become intolerable hours of burning heartbrokenness. To have travailed utterly for this, so long.

John Masefield wrote such words in one of his poems, praying for death. Reaching for the book in which I knew they were to be found, and to read his last lines, I found instead, those of Albert Schweitzer.

STATEMENT OF CASE: ROSEBAY WILLOW HERB

'It is a rude commencement,' he says, 'to unclothe the soul, unless some serious need makes it necessary.' He speaks of *Ehrfurcht vor dem Leben*... 'Reverence... for the private thoughts and feelings OF THE HUMAN SOUL'

'The Soul, too, needs its clothing' ... When he went to the Dean of the faculty, to give his name as a student, he would have liked best to hand him over to his colleague in the psychiatric department, he was told.

To this molestation of mind and spirit there is no end. The mind becomes ill from it, as well as the soul.

The next two winters I spent up the mountain I was so much more ill than before I went. I was to learn the intensity of tiredness was through the high radiation in the mountain to which I had no resilience. My blood was a hundred percent electrical instead of electromagnetic. I could not breathe nor suffer the fumes of the daytime which gathered like a vortex round the granite and stone. It was not sanatorium air. I was imprisoned in the tiredness. There was no visit from the doctor, or even the district nurse.

On Christmas week I had listened to a version of Pilgrims' Progress with John Gielgud as the narrator, a transmission first made in 1947 with musical interludes.

The long winter months dragged on. My birthday was to come. And the next Easter. Easter with crowds of the visitors that were to arrive in the shattered quiet. It was an unendurable suffering.

Summertime brought an intensifying heat which my long windows and casement reflected insufferably. Keeping my curtains drawn and windows open, I struggled to breathe, shivering in all the heat just the same. Sometimes I would have to leave for the fields. There I would lie for part of the day among the sheep, where the May trees or beech offered some shade. On mounds and hummocks I would feel the heat beneath my feet and in seconds little ants were running all over them. The days and nights were lived to the constant cries of the lambs. Daily they would be driven with their ewes, crying and bleating for hours in terror, after they were driven.

Towards the end of the summer a lasting quiet would descend and the thornberries appeared. I thought of *Oak, Ash and Thorn*, as read to us by David Davies on children's hour, of Rudyard Kipling.

Conscious of the woodland spirits and those of bush and briar, I would leave these reluctantly to return, climbing my wooden staircase to balcony entrance through my casement windows.

The air was replenishing again in the last few weeks of summer, but then turned to a sourness as rain deluged down through autumnal leaves, drowning any mellowness. One or two golden sunsets closed final days, as I looked out across the expanse of sea to the island, as it stretched from the view at home, sending down there my evening prayers.

Medical certificates were left at the chemist or surgery when needed to be collected. I had met Elsie Harrison on the side stairs one day, as I came up with my two pints of milk, and she asked me what I was doing out of bed.

When I answered her that the doctor never came, she went down to the surgery herself. Elsie and Bill Harrison had been wardens of the grounds when I had first stayed there so very many years before, but given in their notice, living on independently upstairs. She collected medical certificates each six months for me after that until I decided to make a visit to a new doctor, Robin Williams.

Doctor Williams immediately told me he believed in the myalgic viral infection which had been confirmed for me, but to which there had been such in difference, and that he would be glad to read any research I could give him. Clearly, he knew there was much of this being done. But if I was to believe this would vindicate the many unhappy years there had been then, I was to be very wrong. I told him the changes in housing benefit from the DSS to council offices had meant frequent maladministration , making the wrongs which had to be contended with far worse. The undermining of resistance is a constantly diminishing one.

Hope and confidence in some newfound help turned to dismantled nervous disintegration the following January when a 'nerve-specialist' arrived and knocked on my landing door one Saturday morning. Ultimately I was to come to write of all this. In letters to many.

10. Return To The Hillside Home & Last Farewell To Heidi

In the following summer, I made my first visit down to Penmaenmawr to the chemist, walking to the wicket gate and going down through the field, sitting for a while on my way, to rest, until I reached the waterfall where the little bus ran down the hill twice in the mornings.

I walked from the corner to the chemist and thankfully sat on the chair by the prescription counter. Mr Hollas, the chemist, had in the past spoken to the doctor on my behalf, but none had wondered or held concern at my disappearance, and my mother being alone. To my horror, no sooner had I been sitting for a moment than the door opened and the pitiful sound of her voice struggling in on her stick, cried out, "Can you help me?" she had her back pain, wanted some tablets, had no purse on her, and was altogether distressed. Knowing no more tablets were going to be good for her, the lady behind the counter looked at me!

"I will take her home," I said, realising that was needed of me.

As the driver of the lift I telephoned for, pulled up, the near neighbour to us came out to help. I learnt she had been twice in hospital with her wrist broken, and I was told, her hip, by Eileen Kennish. But why had nobody come up to me! She herself knew I was ill up there, and had turned to look in the other direction when walking her dog, and the car taking me back up the long drive-way, on one day had met her with Ivy's little dog which she used to walk.

My mother recovered herself and we had a drink of tea, but I had been horrified a second time to be greeted by our elderly sheepdog who had plodded to the doorway to me. When my father died she suddenly became old herself it seemed, sleeping much, and I realised she was not well because of her kidneys. I had asked the vet to call while my mother was with my aunty for a few days. The Denes tablets I had been giving her were all used, so he gave me a supply which, he said, were similar. She was to have fish as much as possible, and tripe. My trouble to get the best I could for her, which meant going into Conwy, and gathering all the wild mustard I could from across the road to put into her food, was undone by the determined interference of the evangelical woman, so much to become a thorn in my heart.

I therefore found her in the most dreadful state, her coat matted, her ears black with canker, and her poor, poor eyes suffering the inevitable glaucoma. As we drank tea, my mother put her down a handful of biscuits. Feeding her too much had not helped her condition, and I could have burst into tears at the state of her long sheepdog's coat matted down her back legs. The house was terrible. The hideous fears I had known, that had made me go to the consultant in such desperation, were consummately realised.

My mother went from the table and up to my bedroom for a moment, then returned saying she had put on the electric blanket to air the bed. I looked up the garden from the sunny room we had sat in so often, at the same table, in convivial moments, my heart full. The phone rang and at the same time the door opened and in walked the home-care woman who by this time was coming daily at lunchtime. My mother introduced me as her daughter. Julie Lace was considerate and kind and not of the familiar, as so many are, respecting personal privacy things. But of my mother having a daughter up the mountain she knew nothing. Neither did the new next door neighbours half way up the garden, Margaret Watts and her husband having moved further up, I discovered. Two days on, David Birch came down the garden as I was in the conservatory. "I've mown the grass a couple of times for your mother he said. "I'm with my mum, and we wondered, when your mother said she had a daughter in Switzerland."

Was that what my remote endurance had been? An absence in Switzerland?

My brother had made one or two visits since they had lived there. He had been heard answering my mother about the hedge. Would he cut it? He had not come up to do jobs for her. I knew these were duty visits, but I knew, too, how her manner could change.

She had answered the phone when it rang and this complete transference happened while she was listening to his conversation. And I 'had turned up out of the blue.'

There had been so many intervals when I had not lived at home, for the unhappy reasons I bore in my heart. None more so than this two year interval. My mind couldn't take any more hurt. But it was to go on. And on.

* * *

My mother seemed to think my role was to be there one moment and the next that her home-care visitor was there, and she constantly changed between the two. Julie was kind, and touched me on the arm. "Look after yourself," she said as she went.

Unhappily she wasn't to stay my mother's visiting lady, having to go into hospital herself in a few weeks. There were relief home-visits, one of whom became her permanent home-carer, Pat Stock. And there was the manager Myfanwy Jones, who, visiting to find out whether I was there to stay, caused more of the harrowing unhappiness I was to undergo.

I talked to her about the condition of the home. She did not have an immediate reply, but then said, "Well, we are carers, not Cleaners."

* * *

Heidi's condition was breaking my heart, and I knew she needed her life brought to a gentle close. It was then that my mother told me, Doctor Hutt had arranged for her to go into the residential home but that she hadn't wanted to put Heidi to sleep. Eileen Kemish reiterated this. My mother had become too much of a neighbourly problem, it was clear by this time. The corner couple opposite were still friendly however, to my undying thanks in the not too far distant future.

I had to make return visits back up the mountain when these times were too much, and my mother's turns of inconstancy meant conflict with the instructions being given by the home-care manageress. These incidents were clearly relayed back the whole time (to her), in the most disloyal way. I knew Julie Lace would not be doing this. Further to this, was the persistence of the evangelical woman, and my brokenheartedness over Heidi, and I decided to telephone the vicar. *Has he not wondered where I have been?* I thought.

He came round within the hour, just after six, and I unburdened to him the kind of time I had been having. He urgently said he was going to go round to Doctor Robin's house. Dr Anne Ellis had bought the big house at the top of the garden, but she had been dismissive when newly joining the practice.

Dr Nefyn, a further new partner turned up the following afternoon, a Saturday, and wanted to know *what it was all about*, meaning Dr Robin's visit from the vicar. I told him he should be asking Dr Robin, and that it was to him the vicar had gone. This was the first encounter with, or time I had met Dr Nefyn Williams. And there was to be another, Dr Mark Walker, all of whom seemed to step in whenever help was asked.

A visit was intended by my brother in November, and Pat Stock was all agog. "I'm looking forward to meeting him," she exuberantly had said. She had also mentioned private care, something home-care workers from the Social Services are always encouraged to do. And she knew that she had some strings to pull.

My brother had disdained my presence at home for many years, coming back from his travels with more worldly scorn visit by visit. These had been at long intervals before, but his letters hadn't. I was to come across some instructions he had given his parents when I had been typing letters for my father to the housing associations when they had their names put down to move back to Surrey or Hampshire. My return, for them to make their decision to move down to *his* house in 1983, had been intended so much as a goodbye visit to this hillside home. I was instead once more a dependant daughter. He was to tell the social services I was living on their pension!

My brother duly came, and spent most of his time at Pat Stock's house, and that of a man she had got in to cut the lawn, Tony Chappell.

"Where is he?" my mother was asking. In between her contrary bouts of demeanour, her regard for me and concern was an act of grace. But it was all too changeable. Furtive things were happening, and because of Heidi my last reserves were spent, I was to know the winter from February onwards of burnt-out mind, back up the mountain.

* * *

In September, towards the end of that previous summer I knew Heidi's condition could not be allowed to continue. The driver I sent for from Llanfairfechan called the morning I sent for him and carried her into the car. I could no longer continue to keep helping her to stand up and she couldn't do her toilet unaided, asking at the door to go out, as she was used to doing before the dreadful situation deteriorated so much that my mother was taking no notice.

How the home-care woman (and her stand-in on days she did not come), had let such a state go on I could not believe. The driver had made special visits to Conwy for her fish diet, but on pleading with the evangelical woman that if she wished to help, she could do the same, she thrust St Paul of Tarsus at me saying that "Everything Jesus had blessed was fit to be eaten." But I could not myself ever pass a butcher's open shop without leaving a passing blessing for the hens or rabbits hung up, or the carcasses of once living sheep or herds that graced the fields and countryside whom I loved so much.

At the vets', he said it was time for Heidi to be released from this state. Feeling I could not go home without her, I arranged for the vet to come to the house at six o'clock at the end of the afternoon.

Taking her home, it was explained to my mother, and helping Heidi onto her feet again, she walked to the door and asked to go out into the fresh air. The home itself was stultifying. Holding my coat belt underneath her to support her weight, she went to the side gate and we walked across to the grass verge the other side of the road for a while. Presently, she picked up one of her many sticks, and laid it at my feet in a playful gesture...

Back indoors, the home-care woman arrived. All the talking and persuasion of the previous hour was then suddenly for nothing. My mother was not going to let Heidi go.

When the telephone rang, it was a doctor, Bill Creaney, he announced. He had been contacted by the surgery. He asked if he could call and visit that hour. I was exhausted and desperately in need of rest after that morning. But I felt it might be some help for the desperate situation.

Dr Creaney arrived with two students and asked if he could take notes during which time Heidi lay under the table at my feet. At the end of his interview there was to be no assistance at all to resolve the dire need for moral direction and no help whatsoever was forthcoming.

Days later I got a copy of a letter he had written, saying in conclusion that I seemed to have 'certain paranoid ideologies.' Without hesitation or delay I took the letter down to the surgery. Dr Robin took one look at it and then said that they *would not come again*. And that he had never agreed to students visiting. I was left utterly and completely emaciated, too much so to even get back up the hill. A local driver from Penmaenmawr had to take me back.

Following this it became untenable to remain in the house, with Pat Stock standing over me while I tried, again, to help Heidi to stand up - each time, saying, "It will break you."

Inevitably, I had to go back up the mountain, even if it was for 48 hours, a chance to rest and gain respite. My hillside neighbour helped me, footfall by footfall, by this time in a heavy fall of snow, to walk the merciless hillside. I climbed the last part of it on my hands and knees.

But it was not to be only 48 hours respite... It was to be nearly nine months before I could go back down the mountain to the hillside home again. My neighbour, David Birch came up to report in

March that Heidi had *gone*. My mother's visitor from time to time, Alma, had called in the vet. To even imagine what the suffering must have been like for her was unendurable

* * *

Running some water from the bath tap some while later, I suddenly saw her, running and at the same time, looking back at me, as she sprang over the brook to the west of the hillside between some bent trees leaning over it. And I knew, thankfully, and gratefully, that she was a young dog again, and that she was in her heaven.

* * *

Heidi's death had come in the weeks on the way to Good Friday, the same travailing of sorrow and the heart's pain I had known in the tragedy of my dear Puss, lived through nearly seventeen years before.

But then I was not incarcerated in these walls. There was grass to step on, and the wet scent of the flowering currant when it rained, and the lovely willows unpollarded then.

The intense tiredness, I had learned, was through the immense radiation contained in the granite. This was of no interest to the visits sent in from Dr Healey's clinic, nor the 'nerve' man Dr Robin Williams had sent, after my two fingers were nearly severed the morning I had tried to collect my letters from the desk downstairs by Dave Allen's crony. The sense of disloyalty by the home-care, so firmly entrenched by now with my mother, with my brother's telephone number to hand in Devon, and the encouragement my mother should pay privately for care, left me incensed with grief.

Whenever I returned it upset her apple cart and she would demand to know how long I was staying! The Vicar, dear Berw, had had words with her that temporarily changed this outwardly, and the home-care manageress had been informed of his concern on my behalf. His words had also gone to the relief home-care, Joan Williams, who, regarding Pat Stock's visits, ventured to say, "We are not exactly bosom friends, you know."

She was, to her also, 'completely without compassion,' and I took this to be in regard to other care visits she made. Joan Williams' instructions from the home-care manageress, however, were also to be without compassion. Views she may have held with any regards to myself were never upheld.

The legal intervention I finally decided I must have was to come further on. In the meanwhile, I suffered that Easter, in away only described in the words of a short story, read in lilting Irish, of a small boy's visits to his church and his conversations held there, alone, with 'the figure on the cross':

"When were you most unhappy?" he had asked Christ.

"Once... In a garden full of rocks..." was the answer. "When some soldiers came round me, and a man I loved very much bent down to kiss me.

"Then... My heart broke... like an eggshell."

For some reason, when I was standing on the bottom stair and Pat Stock was leaving, she reached up, tall as she was, making us at shoulder level, and left a passing kiss, on my cheek.

In sickening fear, my heart, rising, turned over, and I went to lie faintly on the bed.

* * *

Need of respite drove me back up the mountain where I lay in fever.

I was fevered with white-heat of pain in my muscles from lifting Heidi. And each effort to go down for two days milk or letters to the entrance hall, in my weeks of endurance through the summer to come, brought it back.

I tried to spend some days in the field. By August I could bear in my heart no longer, my non-return through denial of Dr Anne Ellis to send the district nurse.

"You can walk, Miss Fairland... You can walk."

She had denied any belief in the reality of ME. The large house above us, now belonging to her after Merryweathers living there for so many years, my neighbour David Birch, had gone round to Her himself.

It had been the vicar who said she had bought it. I decided to telephone the vicarage again. He was away on holiday and standing on my legs at the telephone, I was crying in the end, when I eventually got on answer from the curate John Harvey.

In a couple of hours he and his wife were up there, and I imparted to them everything I had told the vicar. John thanked me for the trust I had in doing this, saying, "Your trust will be honoured." I was not to see or hear anything more that month.

I telephoned John Harvey a second time and he was sorry for the interval that had taken place. He understood my unhappiness. *They had been away on an autumn holiday.*

His second visit was in the company of a clergyman from the diocese who dealt with forms of distress which followed bereavement, which it was implied would meet the needs of which I had made confidence. I had told the vicar the winter before of Nashdom Abbey, and that I had, many years previously seen a photograph of this with a picture of Dom Robert Petitpierre amongst a group of the brothers from this Order in the Church Times on the counter of the Jacks' stationers on the Pant yr Avon. I thought this couldn't be coincidence. I head read of those in distress through dark times being given help from this wonderfully gifted and understanding man. The description of this I had also given to Dr Robin Williams, in view of the vicar's visit to him, and my distress with the evangelical presence as Heidi became more ill. In the course of the conversation on this second visit, however, I realised it registered nothing. Only my desperation made impression. And the parting comment of this cleric was that he would get John Harvey to go down to see Dr Williams. I knew by this, it would do no good at all.

There was one more visit from John Harvey. He informed me that Dr Robin Williams was terribly concerned to help - and they were going to send the psychiatrist back!

I cried out that I wanted help and not punishment. And that it was time I had it. I had described the visit of the 'nerve' specialist through Dr Robin Williams, and what it was like have that grey apparition in upon me, as I had detailed it in writing. Never again, was I going to suffer this. When he had gone I could no longer bear to be by myself, nor in that room, despite my picture of Aslan by the curtain. Despite the weakening traumatic passing away of all that year, I fled.

11. A Baby Comes Into Our Lives

I met my mother just leaving, with a letter to post in her hand. As though nothing of this empty time had passed, she said, feebly, "Oh, I'm just going to post this to David, he's had a new baby."

She came back from the post and told me it was a baby girl that he was going to bring in a few weeks time to see us, and that her mother had helped, to get over Jane's parting. He had been with Jane for some time, living in the Forest of Dean, and studying further for flying training, a decision he had determinedly made. He had led expeditions through nearly every country, and wanted a future he believed more secured this way. He had taught Anne, the baby's mother at the flying club in Exeter. She was employed by a legal firm.

I learnt this when they came six weeks on. The house, as before, was in a horrible state. I did all I could to prepare it for this new baby and to make a welcome feel for the mother we had never seen. I had written to her with a photograph of my baby brother to compare the likeness. It had been said, instantly, however, she was like me, by Pat Stock. Her seeing this resemblance meant I placed in her fresh trust.

* * *

It was a few days after the first news her photograph had come, taken in the hospital just after she was born. Tightly curled little fingers, and fast asleep, her little face reflected the maturity and ageless wisdom that certain babies sometimes have.

My brother let my mother know they were coming up to introduce her and her mother as soon as they could travel. She had been born six weeks early. I sent a letter of welcome with my little brother's photograph. There were clear resemblances, I thought, to my brother as well in her.

I had spent nearly eight weeks by November restoring the condition of the home, the home-care woman providing shopping merely and my mother's dinner, which was insisted upon. My mother continued to say she had never sent for them. They just came, she had said. Of course they had. The permanence of Pat Stock seemed firmly established. She had had instructions clearly, and was 'looking forward' to meeting my brother, the baby, and her mother. My mother had, at some stage, signed her consent to my brother's power of attorney. The duty visits had been regularly since my father died, and telephone calls once a month.

The relief home-care woman was to be coming the day she arrived, Joan Williams. "Would you like some help?" she had asked me, in preparing lunch.

I had said, "Yes," gladly. She must nevertheless have been instructed otherwise. I was, by the time they came, tired. They came in and I asked if they would like to go up to the bedroom. My mother indicated the sitting-room doorway at the same time, so barely acknowledging me, they went in. No greeting did I receive myself, nor thank you for my welcome letter. The baby nestled into the crook of her mother's arm and later, in the bedroom, we talked briefly. They were to sleep in my bedroom for the night. And I returned up the mountain.

* * *

My brother came up to fetch me the next morning before they

left. We sat at the kitchen table for a while and I asked if they were staying with the same friends in Shrewsbury that they had spent the night with on the way.

She said they were, and that the husband was the assistant vicar in a large parish there, but that the vicar himself was so insensitive that he had been sick with clinical depression for six months.

I asked if she was close to her own mother. "Yes," she had also said, and since the birth of the baby, her father too. I knew the depths of my own times of mind-illness would take a terribly long time for her to plumb, and their cause. *But would it ever, one day*, I thought, *be truly possible?*

We waved goodbye, and I thought if I had not a sister-in-law, I may have a sister-in-kind, seventeen years younger.

We received a notification some time on that she was to be christened. They had called her Alexandra.

* * *

I had been informed by Pat Stock that (Anne Bellchambers, the baby's mother) knew of the ME from which I had suffered so much, although my brother hadn't heard of it. She was, she said, much more informed. The viral infection so linked to the poliomyelitis virus, and to the measles, impairs the hormonal chemistry of the blood, besides, as I was to later learn, the geopathic conditions, which can seriously do so as well.

This, I knew, was responsible for the worsening of my back pain when we had moved house at the end of my childhood, and ultimately two years on, the onset of the tiredness and trauma to my immune system.

It was all I was to go through that taught me this. And it was from the kindness of the research scientist, head of Earth radiation and research, who was to send me his papers, Alf Riggs. All of which was to come.

* * *

Some twelve days went by from their departure, and my mother pronounced with her coat and bonnet on that she was going down to the village. I have no memory of whether she said it was for the proverbial bottle of sherry or not, but since we no longer had my father's homemade wine, this had become a regular errand, sometimes telling me beforehand that it would be a tonic for me, and would do me good! The unhappy part of this was, that it would do the reverse, as I had no alcohol tolerance and sadly could never enjoy the beautifully made home-wine which for years my father had made with her.

I had had to find my mother's money in the house so many times, that it had become worrying also that she had kept going down to the bank and for no reason withdrawing it. On asking me one day to put something away in her handbag for her. I found one hundred and twenty pounds in it. Mere days before we had searched in vain everywhere for her pension book. These searches were always going on. I came to understand this in the aftermath of her death. My own trauma made the same thing happen to me, for a long time. I repaid the money into the bank for her however, explaining what had happened.

My brother, deciding to put into Pat Stock's hands as much responsibility as he could gave her charge of running my mother's accounts and informed the bank, he was putting a twenty pound limit upon any withdrawals she had made. He had, of course, persuaded her into giving him this discretion to instruct on her behalf. He handed to me his written instructions so that I should clearly understand this and made it very clear that Anne, the baby's mother, was his solicitor.

She was not my mother's, she was not mine, but it was to become plain what intentions were in hand, I painfully realised, looking back upon this time. But I realised it little then. It would have made no difference if I had upon the consequences.

My mother duly returned with the bottle of sherry on the aforementioned morning in demeanour completely at variance to that with which she had gone. Upon her return, Pat Stock had come, and tried to get her to desist; which she refused to do. The presence of the two of us together in the house always meant this variance would come about. Something I was later told to be atypical of the mind's deterioration in this way. I knew nothing at this time of the recording

STATEMENT OF CASE: ROSEBAY WILLOW HERB

tapes which could be dialled for information and that doctors and social workers should be prevailed upon for management of this condition and help towards the relatives. Had they not been prevailed upon enough. Twenty years of prevailing had to be described in the end to the Community Health Council, and they refused, four years on, not only to have any kind of meeting which the Health Authority's Mr Hardie tried to negotiate, but he was, in January of 1997, dismissed from their services. Or, as it was put at the time, he took early retirement.

Description was made of everything that happened this day. I telephoned the surgery upon my mother once more falling on the bedroom floor, and insisted upon the doctor coming to the house, then. Not, I had said, in two hours or more. Then.

What I had not bargained for was her being taken into the Conwy Old Hospital into the rehabilitation ward, where I had to visit for the next month, utterly deserted of all home-care help and left with the unbelievable amount of washing I found, which should have been taken. It had been conceded, I myself should be receiving the home-care help I had never been given on the instructions of the hospital in 1987. I now, had the cost, from my meagre benefit, of visiting the hospital every two days with a couple of visits in the company of Alma, who had not taken my mother to church, for understandable reasons, for some time. Nearest to us, Eileen Kemish, had told me I had given her the kiss of death - I was incredibly upset, and I thanked the sister on the ward, Sister Cook, from the bottom of my heart when she said it was the best thing I had ever done for her.

My brother thought otherwise, however, and there was no moral upholding from their direction whatsoever. I had had to phone Anne Bellchambers' parents in Kent, in the end with the news, as the airport at Exeter had passed me on to her number. Pouring my unhappiness at the harrowing deterioration in the condition of the home, all she said was, "It's not your home, it's your mother's."

I went to the hospital on Christmas day. The sister invited me to stay. By the time I left in the evening, not only was I tired, but the lights in the ward gave me the most violent pain in my head, still with me when I went again, the day after Boxing Day. It was heartbreaking each time I had to leave, for I felt my mother now so vulnerable. If only I could look after her, and be helped to in some beneficial way at home.

I was promised a meeting with the geriatrician, Dr O'Burn. It never happened. Ultimately I spent the morning telephoning, his secretary promised he would telephone back but he didn't. I rang again, and again. Finally he telephoned to speak to me, and his demolition job done, I lay wretched, convulsively.

I could not stay in the house. The nursing officer, Mr Roberts, pulled his chair up in the corridor and sat talking with me, putting me back together, until I went, broken-up but calmly, back into the dayroom where they all sat, my mother among them, for the remainder of the two hours, until once more, the time for my leave of her came.

In the remaining two weeks she asked to go to bed each time I had gone home. And on the days when I would phone in between, I would be told she had asked to go to bed at five. "She was tired."

Not a single hint was there that she was to be diagnosed with dementia. Not even then.

It was with less than twenty-four hours notice they phoned up to say they were sending her home. They could not keep her any longer. She kept trying to get on a bus! I was desperate for the meeting with the hospital social worker that never happened. No almoners anymore, just the hospital social worker. And I was incredulous they would be so insensitive as to come together, the home-care manageress, Myfanwy Jones with her, and sit and talk in front of my mother about her and the arrangements for Pat Stock's return.

I mentioned that in order for my mother to have a change she should come up to me every second day or so, but it would help for her to spend a few hours under some caring vigilance if this could be done. The most important thing being to prevent the trips down the hill again, and the undoing of her month's rest. It would not be contemplated, I was told! When I phoned the surgery it was again, the terse Dr Mark Walker, who had come to the house when I had demanded four weeks before. I was told there was no needed for my mother to have any vigilance. There was no problem!

I do not remember how many days passed by following the demoralising knowledge there was to be no more of the upholding that hospital Sister Cook had given me, but my mother did manage to unfix all the radiator knobs within a very little while when she returned home. These I had had fixed. She would fiddle with any knobs, including the television which was constantly without a picture. As soon as it was corrected, she would fiddle again. And it would go wrong. The home was airless and the heat unbearable in the rooms. The heat so burned the paint that the front radiator knob jammed and could not be turned down. She remedied it. With incredible strength and using the secateurs she removed the knob!

I had help I could never have been more thankful for from neighbours on the corner opposite, Dolly and George. The carpet turned back, the furniture moved, telephone directories were pushed underneath to soak up the pool that readily soaked a large part of it, and rags were tied round the leaking thermostat. For days this went on, until one morning my mother suddenly decided, peeved, that she was tired of this upheaval and wished she had not come home.

I reasoned with her, that much trouble had been gone, to come to our help, and no blame had been made. "We must be grateful," and I received her retort.

"Look who's paying for it."

It was not my mother who had paid for it. I had handed cash to the plumber, nevertheless asking for a receipt in my mother's name. It was immaterial to me. I wore the role of daughter in the home, and I could only pray for sufficient grace to carry on.

The doctor was in again, however, half-way through the morning. In Pat Stock's presence he asked my mother who she wanted to look after her. This was doctor Nevin. Pat Stock knelt down. Taking my mother's hand in hers, she said "It's me, you want isn't it."

My mother did not directly reply to this, but pouted. The doctor, this time Nefyn Williams, this time looked at me and said, "When is the psychiatrist next going to come?"

* * *

A neurologist, writing about this ME ended his description by saying, "There is nothing this disease does not take from you... Nothing!"

Doctor Nefyn, besides others I had talked to, were light years from knowing what this meant.

* * *

I fled from this utter denial of upholding to me, which was just, as I realised, what the home-care, and also what the doctors wanted. The agonising year gave me the most intense worsening of the pain in my right eye, the damage here being, I knew, long sustained in the temporal lobe. I did not think I would live a winter more. Believing this now, I decided on a final note to my aunt, and that a touching bequest, some while before from Great Aunt Lil, should go to the dear baby, whose first birthday would fall then...

I sent to my aunty Mary, what was, in writing it, a goodbye letter. I hoped in the course of time she would realise this is what it had been. The demoralisation I felt through the ME campaign and the failure of the legal indemnity I had believed and hoped on the horizon I withdrew the remainder of Aunt Lil's gift and sent it in cash giving J.W. Hughes name c/o. And I addressed it to little Alexandra. I had put aside for her five or ten pounds at a time, a little each week. Putting this together, this and my aunt's letter were posted.

The beginning of this winter found me at breaking point with Dr Nefyn Williams and I decided I would go to the Conwy solicitors who already had a background since my father's death, of my circumstances, and my having to leave the mildewed rooms I had been living in and go up the mountain. They said they could not represent me then, as they had acted for the owner, David Thornley, in the past, but that they regretted the whole *unfortunate matter*. They knew how challenged I was by the endurance of living there... But I was given none of the help or representation which I needed.

I learnt of the new doctor at the surgery practice, Robin Williams and decided to go to him. Following my visit the surgery sent me, on his instruction, forms for Disability Living Allowance. The first medical report to claim this was written by Dr Tudor Owen in Conwy, the traditional family doctor. He asked how I had come and how I was.

I said that I struggled to breathe more than to walk and that I had an unventilated landing, and there was always cigarette smoke to breathe permeating through the partition and skirting of my bedroom and bathroom and my own entrance. The heavy sash windows were a strain to open and close which I had to do constantly, standing on the windowsill. I had to close them against the fumes from vehicles below and the estate wagon driving round, which would stand with the engine running while the dustbins were emptied beneath the trees on the bank. Some days these fumes clung to the building and it seemed far from sanatorium air.

For some time there was drilling work to make a new veranda below and tar-pitch being melted for some roofing work, all of which choked me. The worst of it was, that I could not breathe with my windows closed. I did not know then it could be the lindane used when the staircase, which had been at the end of the landing, was burnt down, The partition then between my bedroom and those rooms at the front seemed made of cardboard, so strong were the smoke fumes or the burning smell of cooking. It was in these rooms that the rehabilitated workers lived whose taunting I had to withstand. The toilet cistern would sometimes be pulled incessantly at night. I could not stand the pain of it. I couldn't stand the council worries. I spent all my days contending with letters to them or David Thornley.

The details had been to J.W. Hughes in vain. Dr Tudor Owen insisted that I should make a visit to the MP Wyn Roberts. Wyn Roberts abysmally failed to have any interest whatsoever and my report from Dr Tudor Owen was turned down by the DSS. I thought the solicitors would now hold some concern towards this continuing trauma. After a further refusal, I then received a letter asking me to visit Sarah Helm who was articled to the firm. She reviewed the circumstances and especially that of the social services welfare. "I will write to them," she said.

In my hopes that this would lead to some definite upholding to me I was wrong. She was taken off my case to attend to a police enquiry, a wasted hour being spent waiting for her on a fourth visit while she was in the police station where she told me, "I have to go back."

I duly received a letter following this, referring me to a Michael Baker of Swaine, Johnson & Wight in Denbigh. He dealt I was told, with cases of mental cruelty.

* * *

Alma paid a visit to my mother and I, on her coming home from hospital and listened to this verdict. Concerned, she said something should be done. Some twenty minutes after she went the telephone rang. "I will take you to Denbigh," she said.

I had written to Mr Thomas in J.W. Hughes in November. It took until 14th March to go to see the solicitor in whom I thought some hope might lie. And it was at two o'clock in the afternoon, once again, in the rest time I wasn't able to have The car journey gave me pains in my legs and I was fourteen hours with the cramping afterwards that prevented sleep. I was immensely grateful to Alma, however, for taking me.

* * *

I wished the pain of this travelling time had been understood by Michael Baker who had seen me. Looking at some of the material I had taken him, he had said that it 'looked as though some investigation into medical negligence was merited.'

Concerning the social services, however, he would have nothing to do with them, or the DSS, and the maladministration of all my housing benefit I had had to take home with me. I had too many problems he had said, for him to be prepared to look into.

Dismayed utterly, that, sick as I was, I had had to have all the repeated problems with the rent payments unpaid or delayed to me, and the increases in rent and threatening letters from David Thornley (since my words with the Welsh Tourist Board when their visitors came round in May 1990). I asked Alma if I could leave all this with Jack Davis, local JP which duly he received off me on the way home. Jack said he would look at them and deal with the Council but this wasn't to happen, finally, and five months on he returned them all to me.

Anne Brooks, secretary at Craig Lwyd Hall, had typed out every one of the letters I had had, unsympathetic since the very day my father had died, and my time in the home with, my mother had become so unhappily and frighteningly worse. Only on Heidi's death had she mellowed temporarily.

Two days after my visit to Michael Baker, I received a letter 'warning' me he would not look into the many problems I had, but

STATEMENT OF CASE: ROSEBAY WILLOW HERB

would let me know when he had considered the case for negligence.

My return up the mountain was inevitable, and I missed the vital life-line I did not have of the telephone upstairs. The tone of Michael Baker's letter left me feeling I would hear no more from him.

It was exactly ten weeks later when a letter arrived one morning, together with an envelope from the ME Campaign. Mr Baker was sorry for the delay in writing, but it was clear I had had a 'torrid' time. If I would confirm my former conversation with him, he would begin the procedure of investigating the case for medical negligence in this disease pathology known as ME.

The second letter with this was the news of Martin's death. Martin Lev, who had, with Sue Finley and Dr Anne MacIntyre, initiated the campaign for ME, and who had so kindly, made a telephone call to me, leaving a message downstairs in the office to ring him, two years before.

This, together with my letter from Michael Baker, meant I answered, unhesitatingly, sending the legal proposal made to me, on to the campaign. I believed this would be the best tribute I could make to Martin, to follow this through, as a precedent for their cause.

I returned to Michael Baker my answer in every desperate way. In the next five weeks there was, in my large and spacious sitting-room, a cameo of light as though shining from a large oval mirror in the centre of the room, out of which he was about to step. Soon after this appeared, it became a double cameo. In the other 'mirror' was the shining image of Harry Edwards, wonderful healer and vigorous campaigner himself, the reassurance lifting my spirits onto the crest of imminent hope of restitution proceedings.

It was only after some passing while of this so all-encompassing certainty that some creeping presentiment began to lessen this. I had no answer from Michael Baker further. I had no answer at all from the ME Campaign. I was to wait six weeks for this, eventually writing again. The reply eventually came that a certain Nick Andersen had taken over as replacement to Martin Lev. And he would answer me when he came back from his holiday!

So much for my case being a precedent for their cause. I couldn't believe the words I read. I read them again. They really didn't want to know! How unreal. How much greater was the unrealness of my life to become?

Eventually Nick Andersen sent an answer, sending two recommendations of doctors for a specialist medical report.

Michael Baker, in the meantime had done nothing. He then sent a letter to Dr David Lewis of Bronglais Hospital, Mid-Wales, and I waited for an answer yet again as to how I was to travel there. Given that my journey to Liverpool had left me irreversibly worse, I had no idea how I was to get there.

After many more weeks I finally decided if Michael Baker wouldn't answer, I would ask Dr David Lewis to. His reply was a last and final anguish.

He knew nothing of a letter from my solicitor. His clinic was an adult diagnostic one, held monthly and he would not get involved in any legal matter. His signature, in a crabbed hand, was written above a note to say he had 'unearthed a letter from my solicitor...' For me, he had written my epitaph.

Little did I know that this disease pathology was not terminal. Little did I know the soul breaking years of living it out which lay still ahead. There was absolutely no communication at all with or from Michael Baker for the rest of that summer, and as my strength ebbed away and the temporal pain in the right side of my head returned more intensely than before, I did not feel there was light ahead towards another spring!

* * *

I resolved in the New Year I would deal myself with the Council Rent Office. I made three visits in January, February, and March to no purpose, the proud and arrogant Miss Valeria Hobson ignoring my wait through her lunchtime on my third.

On the morning I went they had started smelting more roofing-pitch and in a mortar-mixer were throwing in spade-fuls of what looked like cement to do another repair to the roof. There was a cauldron beneath my window and I was literally driven to sending for a lift to go and tell them of the environmental officer's responsibilities. When he refused to do anything about the mildew in my rooms below the hillside, my fate had been sealed for the six years I was sick up in such a remote place.

When called up there to view he merely said that the fire exit sign through my sitting room should not be there and the landing should not be closed off. The Welsh Tourist Board had apparently said the rooms could not be let for tourists for this reason. Why had nothing else been said? Why was not the main staircase rebuilt when it was burnt down? There was no escape for the smoke-filled air. My bedroom was filled with it and my partitioned bathroom. It filtered through the skirting board and up through the floorboards as well, when the cigar smoke would sicken me and I would suffer chokingly, sobbing it all out. Summer braziers were lit below for their suppertime entertainments and my ears would hurt with the decibels of noise more and more and more. My inner right ear became permanently painful. The tendon of my left hand was severely painful as my letters had been snatched out of my hand when collecting them from the reception desk one morning. My correspondence was always interfered with. I was handed three letters one day with the words, 'sorry, we've done it again.' They included my rent cheque for that month torn in half. I finally had my rent paid direct to David Thornley, after delays for six months between October 1989 and March 1990. I still continued to receive letters about these delayed payments from the secretary to David Thornley and they never contacted the rent department themselves. Instead I suddenly had demands for council tax payments which I had made other attempts to get some representation for. The candidate for the Liberal Democrat Party Roger Roberts had made no response to me four years before in my needs for help. This time he came, accompanied by a lady to whom I described my distress and with the reassurance he would write to the magistrate's office, he departed. I received a copy of his letter a month later in which he had informed them that because of my 'great distress I would not be able to make myself coherent in the courtroom.'

I tried to phone Nick Andersen on my February visit to the rent office as the telephone at the Hall entrance was not working. The cashier helped me to get through to the research campaign from her desk telephone. I waited to speak to Nick Andersen and after a considerable silence a stony voice came down the telephone. It was the purpose of the campaign to represent the dependency on benefits for those with ME, now my diagnosis. Case histories were constantly being asked for. It was, with every certainty, this phone call which was responsible for the memorandum eventually to appear on my file with Michael Baker. Quite apart from this, I had filled in a second time for Nick Andersen the questionnaire which was passed on to Dr Ann MacIntyre. This was only vindicated, years later, by Dr Sarah Myhill, writing to my GP by then in the Conwy Practice.

Undeserving of this further instalment of mental cruelty from the campaign I sought to contribute to, I put in writing to Sue Finlay how I felt. It was a long time since the last correspondence I had had with her, describing her trip to France on her husband's behalf, sending me the cuttings from the newspaper.

The increase in the growth of the campaign and all that had made me sicker had prevented it. I thought she would be quite dismayed herself at the betrayal I had been caused. Her not unkind letter, however, was clearly influenced by some of the counselling she by that time must have been given. She replied with the words, "We can't all be victims and rescuers..."

I knew from the wireless programmes I listened to that I was not alone in being sickened by all the modern day psychology we are constantly being fed. The only reply in my heart was that, "I *Am* My Brother's Keeper."

Oh, so sadly have I departed from a church I once loved, and from which reverence has departed.

* * *

My agony of the next twelve months was spelt out ultimately, to the Community Health Council as this is what I was told I should do by the manageress of the CAB. In this time there was published Bryan Kheenan's account of his time held hostage. It was entitled *An Evil Cradling*.

And by Terry Waite, his autobiographical description of his time in captivity, *Taken on Trust*.

* * *

In the year leading up to my writing to the Community Health Council my mother was put into the EMI ward of the local general hospital and succumbed there to the influenza from which she died.

With forty-two pounds a week only, due to further miscalculation of my benefit, I could manage only two journeys a week to the hospital, leaving me ten pounds which was not enough for a third trip and I consequently last saw her fifty one hours before she died. After this, the telephone had a call-bar put on it and I was able to make no further telephone calls to the hospital. I received a letter, delivered by hand by Eileen Kemish, who worked part-time at John Bellis Solicitors, saying that I was a trespasser in the home and my mother had been kept in the ward until I was removed from it.

I had lain on the floor for 24 hours after delivery of the letter, and only then did I telephone Mr Sells, our family solicitor, at his home at Kesteven on the Guildford Road in Woking. With remonstration he said "You are not to leave that home." He was going to look into it, but finally, under warrant for repossession, I was to leave the hillside home under Clause 24 for Vagrants.

How shall the summer arise in joy
Or the summer fruits appear,
Or how shall we gather what griefs destroy
Or bless the mellowing year,
When blasts of winter appear.

- W.M. Blake

* * *

My mother had last looked on me with eyes too frightened and body too trembling to speak. I realised this was the drugs her body was suffering under. My own response to medication I had been given all those years ago had been the reason I had woken up in a hospital bed and gone through the terrible treatment that had happened to me. I understood her frightened condition now. The not understanding what is happening to you, and the reason for the only words she could speak, "Please take me home with you."

They were not the eyes with which she had looked out so firmly two previous evenings before. When I went on the Saturday afternoon she asked me how I had come. "Dad will give you the money," she said. And then, when I had sat by the bed for a while, "Shall we put the kettle on?"

I told the nurse she felt like a cup of tea. When they brought it, she said, "Aren't you having any?" I said I would have a cup when I went back home. She then said, "Yes, and look at the garden." We had a pleasant kitchen and always enjoyed the garden view. I had wanted nothing more than to have taken her home with me in these passing weeks that had seen her get steadily worse.

I said, "I have to look at the garden alone until you come back with me."

With resolution she then said, "No!" As she had raised her head off the pillow. Her 'no' remains a living word. "I will be coming home. I will look at the garden with you. I will be thinking of you while I'm lying here."

She became tired and as I reluctantly left, she looked long and hard into my face, and said as she had many times before, "You've got your Dad's eyes." Lines from 'The Soul's Dark Cottage' came back to me.

The Soul's dark cottage batter'd and decayed

Lets in new Light by chinks that time hath made.

The nurse had wanted to come in at nine, but I wished afterwards I had not gone home.

The hours of Sunday were long, knowing I needed to be with her as much of the time as I could be. But interminably I had to wait until Monday night for my next lift. I was frightened to find her weak and trembling. Strong as she had always been, she pleaded with me again, when she could speak, "Take me home with you."

* * *

"Take me home with you." The last request of hers I could have granted. Her eyes looked as they had done only weeks before when she had come up to get me from Craig Lwyd Hall. It was Sunday and she had 'come to take me home' then. On Monday morning the home-care woman had arrived and she met me with her remonstrance. And too unhappy to remain, I had gone back once more to the lonely endurance I had born up there.

I paid for the times I had made reconciliations with the home-care services with regret too bitter to endure. No healing was there to the injury done to my right arm which caused me to return again. Inconsistencies with my mother made me repeat back to them, "This... cannot go on." On the Monday morning that I returned up the mountain, her eyes had followed me as I went... 'I came up to get you, and yet now you are leaving again.'

The injury to my arm had been one afternoon when at teatime, my mother brought in a photograph saying, "Do you remember this?" It was the garden where I was four years old and with my arm round my baby brother in a deckchair for the photograph. She had made the blue-spotted dress with the sailor collar and she kept the picture in the bookcase. We sat and had tea and she went to put on the news while I went up the garden steps to deadhead the daffodils, and speaking to my neighbour, talked for a time. While up there we noticed the home-care woman, Pat Stock, had returned and was sitting at the tea table earnestly talking to my mother. Suddenly my things were thrown out of the door, my mother cane up the garden steps and told me to go! My neighbour then leapt the fence as she cracked her stick against my arm. She had never done such a thing in her life before. When Alma was sent for, it was her husband who came down and my neighbour's mother came round to help then to take me to the car.

Sitting in a room with the geriatric consultant and Mrs Wendy Lonsdale, with whom I had had such confiding conversations, I was to hear that I had been harming my mother. I said I wished Alma to be present. She and my mother had gone to meetings together for several years and she knew that neither would I harm my mother, nor in her right mind, would my mother harm me. When we returned home she said to me that I had been tried and convicted. But I had had no trial. Not even my turning to the Community Health Council had brought that about, or the manageress of the CAB who had told me to contact them. I had been convicted without trial. My mother was no longer mine to have any rights towards, as when she had been in hospital in Conwy and I had the support of Sister Cook and of Mr Roberts. Whilst there she thought she was staying somewhere at the National Trust. She and my father had been one-time stewards at Clandon Park in Surrey and I still have her notes. But even then I was denied any regard by the consultant, Dr O'Burn, and torn by it I will be forever.

For six weeks she was detained in the hospital until at ten past two on Thursday afternoon, 11th November, she died of the influenza in the ward. It was Remembrance Week. Armistice Day.

When the telephone rang it was for my brother who was asked for by the hospital. I said they were speaking to Me and that my brother was in Devon. They had not kept their promise to me to let me know if my mother became any worse. My brother had apparently been sent for and had been at my mother's bedside with my aunt, but had returned to Devon. I had been in desperation since the call-bar was put on the telephone from Monday night onwards, for I had tried to ring the hospital again as soon as I had got home. I felt more Ill than I knew how to go on, and could only try to claim my rest thinking of my mother in surrounding 'light'. I sent her a small card with a message saying, 'I will be with you in the morning' hoping I would be able to get my lift from a local driver before he did the children's school run. She did not read it. It had said 'I will bind up that which is broken and heal that which is sick.'

It was, in fact, a little card she had once given me.

* * *

I asked to see her. It was a cold night. I was taken in a wheelchair across to the mortuary and there they took their leave of me for a few moments.

I could not find her hands...
They were all wrapped up...
She was all wrapped up...
I could not feel her fingers... Or hold them one last time...

I had taken her wedding ring with me. It had become too loose for her to wear it. She had told me always to keep it, because she had never kept Grandma's . I had taken lotion and cotton wool for her face. There was nothing but to plead for her to be transferred to the Chapel of Rest and to leave with the promise this would be.

The Vicar, however had asked permission for my signature to the death certificate, but it was in vain. My brother, notified in Devon, was made legally responsible for her.

It was not until the Thursday night, at 7 o'clock, and a further seven days after she died, I saw her. Too late for them to have beautified her… Her face was framed in white satin. Her hand held the little card I had sent her, and in her coffin had been scattered my Rosemary.

* * *

Dear Lord and father of mankind,
Forgive our foolish ways;
Reclothe us in our rightful mind;
In purer lives our service find
In deeper reverence, praise
In deeper reverence, praise.

PART III

12. Mr Justice Parry Is In The Dock

"Don't leave the phone," the woman on the dementia helpline had said. "I live only five miles away, I will come and see you." Some months had passed by and I had learned too late of this service. Sylvia Hogan, a nurse who worked with Gwynedd Outreach had spoken to the Social Services on my behalf, as had done the vicar, "But," she had said to me, "in thirty-five years experience with them, they are blind to what they don't want to see and deaf to what they don't want to hear." But it was better than nothing to talk to somebody now. Vascular dementia, I had learned, was a step-wise deterioration that takes place because of a sequence of small strokes in the brain, with times of normality between. How many times would my mother ask if she had done something to upset us? By the end of my father's illness, I would find him down in the garage with the door pulled down, crying behind the car.

No remorse had there been nor visit, after my mother's funeral. And even the yearly Christmas card from Mr Sells never came. Only a letter in February saying that probate had been passed and asking if I wished to buy my brother's half of the home to remain there.

Quite unlawfully, my rooms had been repossessed at Craig Lwyd Hall and notice served to the solicitors in Devon, Anne Bellchambers' legal firm, saying I owed sixteen hundred pounds in rent. Having had the rent registered on repeated increases, I obtained invoiced copies in the end and sent them to my mother and father's solicitors in Woking to pass on.

I told my helpline visitor, Mrs Pamela Day, of the correspondence. And, that I had, by May of 1994 received a letter which entitled me to a medical tribunal, my application having been made so long before.

On telling her this she said that a Welfare Rights Bureau had been set up funded by the Welsh Office in Caenarvon. This funding, however had only lasted for two years which had continued under the Social Services. I rang up and spoke to the most courteous gentleman who said he would come and see me. And from then on proved to be a strength and stay through many of the problems that beset me, despite being far outside his remit.

For one thing he contacted Mr Sells, who said that he was very concerned and sorry that my brother was taking such action against me. I had summons for the telephone, electric, and also for water rates, and had proceeded to pay for a water meter to be put in for my mother before she had died. This was before legislation came in to make it obligatory for water companies to provide meters for households. Finally I received summons for an oil bill for central heating from March onwards, but had persistently replied saying that the boiler had broken down finally on 30th January that year, 1994.

I telephoned the Small Claims Court and said I could not possibly attend. Telling them of the circumstances, they said that my defence could be read in court by the clerk. It was not read out and I was ordered to pay ninety pounds with court costs.

On ringing back to the court I was told then, as though it was all in a matter of course, "Oh, all is not lost, we can book a second hearing."

* * *

I told Mrs Pamela Day about this, and she begged me to contact the manageress of CAB again, who, she said, had a firm voice at

STATEMENT OF CASE: ROSEBAY WILLOW HERB

industrial tribunals and various committees upon which she sat, including Mencap. Her own son was severely autistic. I said my previous experience of the CAB had not been happy.

I therefore duly sent a letter addressed to Mrs Paula Lynch detailing all that had lead up to this arbitrary decision by a Mr Justice Parry. It was some considerable time before I got a reply from her saying she was very sorry but could not help me, in view of the complications leading up to it.

On reading her reply I just sat and put my head on the table. Presently there was a tap on the door, and then Alma came in. Having been present with me when visiting the hospital and the geriatrician when Mrs Wendy Lonsdale was present (the welfare lady who had on a number of visits talked with me), and then having taken me to my mother's funeral, she knew I had written my letter. I handed her the reply. As she read it the phone rang. I just put my head back on the table and she answered it. Mrs Lynch had reread my letter and felt she should speak to me to say my mother's solicitor, Mr Sells should be helping me. Alma's remonstrance included the fact that I had just given up any fairness in view of the rehearing I awaited over the summons.

She was then told that Mrs Lynch would represent me upon my written consent and that she would come and get my signature to attend the rehearing. She obtained spread sheets of various different addresses, three of which, she said, had wide discrepancies. My address was one of the three.

In January, the case was struck out by Mr Justice Griffiths, and the oil company profusely apologised for their error.

This news was followed by Mrs Lynch then telephoning me saying she realised my *security of tenure* in the home was clearly a cause of concern, and that she would make contact with the Trustees and with the Council.

In the December of 1993 just over four weeks following my mother's death, I had had a phone call from the Borough Solicitor, Maria Kells, who had belatedly looked into the handling of all the rent payments to Craig Lwyd Hall and all the distress that had been caused during such an ill time. It was, she said, 'serious harassment and quite unlawful' and I was to have no hesitation in contacting her again if I was distressed any further by it.

If only, if only, her words could have been depended upon. As it was, Mrs Lynch managed to get a written agreement that a payment of rent would be considered to the Trustees in order that my living on in the hillside home could be secure. But of further contact with Maria Kells there was to be none. For she, herself was ill, and consistent absence from her office was the reason she had taken so long to contact me more than a year before.

My suspense and uncertainty of these weeks were heightened by not being able to make contact with Mrs Lynch at all, unless she contacted me. The telephone line only gave the opening times of the office, and when they were open the line was constantly engaged. So it was in shock and distress that, one week after my birthday I got proceedings delivered to me by hand, personally from Brian Cunningham, of John Bellis Solicitors to gain repossession of the hillside home.

* * *

When I *did* manage to speak with Mrs Paula Lynch again, she said it was a *necessary* step. I was to put it under the carpet. I was not to make myself ill over it. She would represent me as she had done before. I was told very differently by the court office.

I decided to ring the BBC Legal Department to find out what they had to say, and was told it was very important for me to be present myself in the court. By the Court Clerk I was told the same. For weeks I tried to contact Mrs Lynch again. Finally, days before the hearing was due on 24th April 1995, she did telephone me. She would come to get my signature for her to represent me, she said. I told her what the BBC and the court clerk had said and to my shock and disbelief, she then said if I was going to be there myself, she had not the time.

It took me four years to find out that the proceeding should have been heard in Chambers and not in Open Court. The court had been booked for the entire day and I had the cost of the journey by car, by myself, all the way to Rhyl Courthouse following Easter of that year.

STATEMENT OF CASE: ROSEBAY WILLOW HERB

* * *

The wait was a long one that morning. I was handed a second set of affidavits as I entered the waiting room by Brian Cunningham. I had already had a copy of these, however, to which I had had to spend the hours typing out the answers to hand to the clerk. They were a set of pages drawn up to 'give a background to the court'. I explained to the Clerk Mrs Riches, that I had been sent a set of these pages already. And that I had answered them. She took them off me. We went into the courtroom at half past twelve.

* * *

Within minutes we returned to the waiting area and were told we would resume at two o'clock when these affidavits and my answers to them had been read. After returning at two o'clock from lunch, Mrs Riches came into the waiting area and said it was 'time to go home!' The case was not going to be heard that day. I was to get a solicitor and a *proper* defence. The Judge did not like the way the proceedings had been served.

* * *

Utterly dismayed that nothing had been resolved after this long journey and tiring and painful morning in my back, the drive back brought me home at just about quarter to four, spent for nothing. I was to get a solicitor. After nine years, how! Four solicitors had been unable to represent me in the seven years between my father and mother's death, because they had acted for David Thornley at Craig Lwyd Hall in the past. The emergency solicitor I had called in had failed me abysmally and so had the law society. So had Maria Kells, so sadly. And so had Paula Lynch.

I went, in the end, to solicitors in Llandudno and to John Blakesley. There was to be a further hearing on May 24th. He said he would go and not to worry. He would handle it. That was not quite to happen.

* * *

John Blakesley had come to visit me and said the allegations in the affidavits, irrelevant as they were, needed to be answered. They were so untruthful, and not 'background to assist the court' at all. Problems were described over the central heating. The boiler leaked oil which would form a pool at the bottom and the smell would be sickening whenever the boiler was on. My mother, however, would fiddle with the switch constantly and on hot summer days had no idea whether she was hot or cold, one day getting the front radiator knob off and throwing cushions out of the window because the room was too warm. So I had the fuse taken out of the switch for me. As soon as the home-care woman learned this, she was on telephone to Devon and, unable to contact my brother until late that night, then used the front door key to walk in with Joan Williams as well as her husband to put the fuse back. As she said my brother had instructed!

Where was the brother I needed all this time, in these years since my father died? Desperately, desperately needed! I could have written my own 'background to assist the Court'.

* * *

Waiting at home to hear the outcome of the proceedings, the telephone rang. The Judge presiding was not the judge on the day in April when we had gone so much in vain to settle the agreement of rent payment with the council to the Trustees for my half of the hillside home. It was, instead, Mr Justice Parry. Why? I had asked. Why was not the presiding Judge in April hearing the matter on this date in May? Why when the previous dismissal of the hearing was because of the way the proceedings had been served, was this background not part of the continuity? Why, when a Judge had dismissed the evidence of a broken down oil boiler and ordered me to pay, was this same man hearing this case now?

Permission had been given for my brother to inspect the house. He would be arriving with Brian Cunningham as his agent, and a young woman from my solicitor's office.

The disruption into the home when their arrival involved my brother opening sideboard doors and drawers, and throwing onto the floor, a little box of tea knives kept with the cutlery. We never ever used them, but I was always allowed to play with them when I was a child. He attempted to take a small puzzle box, he said, "For Alexandra." It contained two little drawers inside once the way had been found for the box to open.

"No," said the young woman. "Nothing must be taken."

With that they took their leave, but picking up the little box I went after them. "Here you are," I said, giving it to the woman to hand on. "Take this for Alexandra."

* * *

There was a Directions Hearing in July. I was allowed to attend. Alma and Brian said they would take me. I had letters from John Blakesley, however by which I was all too distressed, and I replied saying so. His decision was, he then said, that he would have nothing further to do with the case and would write to me saying so. His affidavits arrived and I was distraught.

Mr Justice Parry sat in the Courtroom. After exchanging amused comment with Brian Cunningham Mr Blakesley handed to him his petition: 'To be removed from the Court Record'. Bending down across his desk (his altar...), Mr Justice Parry said, "Of course, I have to grant you this."

I gasped my breath in.. At once, instantaneously, I knew what this meant. It was the fealty of Brotherhood. *The* Brotherhood. That of Freemasonry. I was given three months to find the money to pay for my brother's half of the hillside home. Until October 30th. No stone was left unturned to find this money. But on October 30th a warrant was granted for Repossession of the home built there 25 years before.

I was told by the Welfare Rights Bureau, that on medical grounds I should have a postponement. Through the Shelter Solicitor I was granted four days. In the meantime my brother came to remove belongings from the house having notified the police he intended doing so. And that he would require their presence to prevent a scene. They said he should go back to Devon and wanted to send him there. I said he was entitled to half the contents of the home. It should have been discussed long ago.

He also notified Eileen Kemish who came round and sat with me, unbelieving as I was, that my once little brother was doing this to me. Where was the little boy of so long ago, so sensitive and affectionate. Who ran in crying to my mother one day because the bin men were collecting the dustbins and someone had put out an old box of broken toys. Sitting on the top of the box was an old teddy. He could not speak for his distress but had dragged my mother by the hand down the road. Where was he now! What happened to him all those years ago? Where went he to!

When he had gone and I went upstairs, he had left my bed and things in the bedroom. All the contents of my mother's bedroom were gone. And he took everything except the settee on which we were sitting from the front room.

Left in the kitchen was a blue glass bowl filled with crystals which harmonised geopathic stress, and which had been sent to me by Jaqueline Beacon and David Gillett working in Environmental Harmony.

On leaving and parting from this home for the last time four days later, the elderly gentleman next door came up the driveway holding out his hands. Taking hold of mine, he shook them and said, "I wish you well." At that moment a camera flash went off from a reporter in the road. Somewhere, that moment is on record.

STATEMENT OF CASE: ROSEBAY WILLOW HERB

With my baby brother in the garden. I am four years old.

Lisabeth Rose Fairland

With my dad holding hands beneath the apple blossom.

STATEMENT OF CASE: ROSEBAY WILLOW HERB

Haymaking time in the fields beyond our house.

Baby leverets found under one of the hedges by Geoffrey next door and quickly returned to their nest.

Lisabeth Rose Fairland

A photograph taken for Ivy Benson that belies the unwell years

13. The Days Ahead (& Nights)

It was 32 weeks after the court warrant that I moved into an empty bungalow without a light bulb or any electricity.

There was no answer at all from our hillside neighbour Eileen who held keys; I thought that would enable me to get such belongings as I needed while staying temporarily in the dwelling to which I had been brought. Only the small conservatory my father had built was open where I was able to get one of the two garden beds to sleep on. I had no curtains to put up, nor anything but the tea, bread knife and Horlicks spoon hastily put into the shopping basket on leaving so many months before.

In my head there was the permanent humming noise of the wiring in the room I had spent the eight winter months in. This had been from the electrical box on the water pipes behind the alcove by the bed, and one above the ceiling just above the doorway into the small box room where I had eventually slept on the floor. The vibration through the bedsprings had been too much to bear. It was finally when the welfare housing officer visited me and heard this humming noise, that I was offered, three days later, the dwelling I came to as a halfway house, until returning to the hillside home on payment of rent to the Trustees which the court should have ruled upon, but hadn't. The housing office had seen a documentary programme made by the scientist Alistair Phillips, and had taken seriously the deleterious effect of the electromagnetic fields produced by this wiring. They gave me the address of the research network into the hazards and benefits of radiation. Some time later I was to receive further information from the College at Llandrillo which was published in Sweden. The research and legislation in that country not being matched in the UK. I was also to learn about bioresonance, a way of programming the body's wavelengths or frequencies, or bandwidths as they are also called, to restore the balance that has been impeded.

I had cut a small patch of the long grass to sit in to try to clear my head, but the humming still persisted from all the many weeks I had endured it, and I could not bear coming indoors. From the confinement of eight months I was released from I now had a small narrow and dark kitchen, a front room, a bedroom and a tiny bathroom, and outside a long garden for which I was grateful for the fresh air and freedom. But the heartache and mind hurt only the psalmists words could utter. I had already written all those years before, in my visiting Dr Tony Dickinson in Chester (and his words to me on that day), and my disappointment to follow, 'There is no language but a Cry...' and my cries went on, and on, and on.

* * *

I passed the weeks in the sure belief that the dwelling I had been brought to was to be a half-way house until some return to the hillside home was legally determined. I said so to Jeremy Grant when he told me I could have it for as long as I needed. A kind and sympathetic Welfare Housing Officer. In October Eileen Kemish came down to tell me the hillside home had been sold. She took out of her bag four apples. "Not from your tree," she said. "Your home is gone now." It was Sunday morning and I sat, after she had gone, watching the October sunlight on the linoleum floor inside the doorway, as I was to do in other Autumns and in the other years that were to follow.

STATEMENT OF CASE: ROSEBAY WILLOW HERB

* * *

My hours lying in the room into which I had been put following the departure from the hillside home, bailiff, locksmith and police behind, brought the memory back long back in the bleak half-light of such a November day, of the ward in which I had had to lie with my scarlet fever when I was four, confined there in the little cot I now remember.

Somehow time had closed this gap down the years. It was 3 p.m. and they who had brought me to this lodging had taken their leave, and I was left deserted, bereft, violated, and broken with disbelief.

It was 3rd November 1995, two years after the bereavement of my mother and the Remembrance Day one week later upon which she had died. No more ignominious could have been the circumstances, nor utterly grievous. Nor greater could have been the denials of help, or moral hope. The following week commemorated how this had happened, November 11th. Now it was two weeks after Eileen had left me and November had come again.

It was following this that the programme was broadcast on the Social Services treatment of the elderly. There was more writing to be done. It was to continue until I was spent and spent again, and eventually too crushed to carry on.

14. Not A Healing Journey

As the days went colder and the time was spent more indoors the humming in my head remained unlessed. There was a central heating radiator in the front room that whined whenever it came on, like some sort of radar signal, coming and going, like a beam or searchlight sweeping the sky. From Jeremy Grant I received the information about the research into radiation and electric magnetic fields and I contacted this research network. Two monthly newsletters were issued and I learnt of the Breakspear Hospital and their treatment of those who had suffered exposure to this harm. I already had an article printed in the newspaper of the previous winter which had been left lying in the chair that the elderly proprietor of the lodgings used to sit in where he could chat in the foyer to people going in and out. It had been done with I was told. It described the treatment of a nurse from Broughton Hospital who had suffered from the chemicals in daily use in the hospital, but a refusal by the health authority had been made to fund the same treatment of her eight year old son who had been born with the same symptoms, as she had been carrying him during the time she herself became ill. An anonymous donor had funded the treatment for this little boy according to the newspaper. I had received money from my medical tribunal. I decided to contact the hospital.

* * *

Following my initial telephone call I sent a written medical history as best as I could compile it, but in the weeks of waiting, then resigned myself to receiving no compassionate response or acknowledgment of any kind. By the time I had a telephone call from Dr Jean Monro I was too demoralised to feel my need for help, so dire, could be compensated for by making the journey of 200 miles in so ill a state, and for so indifferent a reply. Nevertheless my suffering was continuing with no relief. At the suggestion of the receptionist at the hospital I contacted St. John's Ambulance, however, my father having been a serving member in Crewe division during the war years at Fodens. Victor Bodger and colleague therefore collected me on a cold March morning just after seven to make the long return journey in a Land Rover ambulance with minimum vehicle suspension and an unsprung stretcher to lie down upon finally when my back pain became too much.

On arriving in Chester, two more relay drivers took over, and for my sake took the route through Nantwich town centre and square, passing Churches Mansions on the way in. Here was where I used to walk along the low wall round the square in front of the church, holding my mother's hand. The cherry trees were in bloom. I did not want to go on, nor leave the town. Here, I knew I could get well again, healed by the saltmine air for which Nantwich was renown. I did not need Breakspear Hospital. I needed this. But Nantwich town council wrote to me saying that they had enough trouble housing their own local residents to consider helping me. And I was to return, for years to come, to a granite mountain.

On reaching the hospital I was by then several hours the worse from the journey, and my drivers helped me in the struggle to walk in. A few minutes after them speaking to the reception desk to let them know I had arrived I was presented with a form to sign, stating that I was agreeing to Dr Monro's consultation fee. I looked at my two drivers, by then friends, and they looked back at me. I had never before met any request of this kind to have to sign for treatment, and certainly Dr Finn had not done so.

With no alternative but to sign this piece of paper I therefore did so, and my drivers and I looked at one another again.

I was then told there was no working lift and the stairs were indicated. There was no way that I could do this. I told them I had made a journey too painful. My head was throbbing mercilessly. All I wanted was relief. I was told I had to climb the stairs.

My state of collapse was not heeded beyond telling my drivers there was a kettle and a kitchen in which to make a cup of tea, when the impossible struggle had been made to the top. I was sat at a table and several pages were put in front of me that I was then told to fill in. This was a questionnaire. What did I have for breakfast, lunch and tea? The lines ran in to one another, my head worse by the minute and I wondered why I wasn't on the floor by now. Holding on to the edge of the table I said, "Why couldn't these forms have been sent to me beforehand?" I could have filled them in at home.

Presently Dr Jean Monro came in. With no apology she sat down, glanced at the pages and told me to lie on the bed. She looked at my appendix scar and at my teeth. "Mercury fillings?" she said. Telling me to get up again she went and sat back at her desk, and looking down, said, "Well, I shall be writing to the health authority to tell them they need funding for treatment."

Incredulously I told her, "I have come here to receive treatment and to pay with my own money. You know this from the telephone conversation I had with you. It is my Medical Tribunal money. It was explained to you"

Crossly she said, "I know you are disappointed, but I must have health authority funding," and she went out.

So this is what I had signed my consultation fee agreement for! To be told this and goodbye! Disbelievingly both my drivers half carried me back to the Land Rover and laid me on as many blankets as they could fold to make me comfortable. Holding my hand for the best part of the back, Sue was near to tears herself. Ian, my other driver drove the miles of return to Chester. I spent the best part of the next nine months in gradually receding pain, which was never entirely to leave me, however, after this terrible ordeal. I had been hours on the rack. And all for the cavalier way she had dealt with me.

STATEMENT OF CASE: ROSEBAY WILLOW HERB

* * *

Tearfully I had telephoned Jas Chanay who had represented me at my medical tribunal and helped me through so many of the legal trauma that had resulted, eventually in my having to make this journey. He knew of the vibrational injury, and straight away he said the Patients' Association should know how I had been treated. They in turn, said that Trading Standards should refer my case back to the hospital. For months onwards this process continued after a visit to me by Mr Braithwaite, who wrote and wrote again and again to the Hertfordshire Health Authority. On one occasion I had a visit from a different colleague saying he had been grateful himself for reading my case file. He had been unwell for several weeks at a time himself, but with no medical diagnosis that his GP could provide. Each time he went back to his office, he said, he became ill again. And finally learnt it was the computer screens that were responsible, and that there was no legislation here in the UK in regard to this growing problem as there was in Sweden.

Finally he then said, "I know what you have been through with regard to the Social Services. I was a social worker once. But I have had colleagues like myself who took their leave. I could not go along with what they do." There was no redress by this time other than going to the Small Claims Court to recover the fee I had paid to Dr Monro, not to mention the money I had paid for the journey. St John's had said they would accept the cost of the petrol. And both my drivers had taken me in their own time.

It was some recognition I wanted of how unfair it had been to allow me to have made this journey. Dr Monro could have said on the telephone that she would be demanding funding, and knew herself, the health authority had none to spare. I was duly to receive the intimidating reply from solicitors acting on her behalf through the BMA that put paid to any further attempt at grieving apology or remorse from this woman. She was clearly without any notion of pity, nor of conscience. Eighteen months later I was invited to become a Friend of Breakspear Hospital. To contribute to a fund for the specialised treatments it provided. And to read accolades from time to time from grateful patients. What of the ones so poorly served as I had been. For them there is no such story.

***

ARTICLE 1 of 3 74 lines

DML 26 Feb 1996 / Red Tape Alert: Fury over treatment delay for poison boy (713)

By CHRISTOPHER BOOKER and RICHARD NORTH

A DOUGHTY House of Lords campaigner for chemical victims is now locked with health officials in the battle to win proper medical care for Mark Griffin, the desperately sick eight-year old boy who for months has been in a Hertfordshire hospital, waiting for officials to agree funding for his treatment.

We have reported several times on the red tape nightmare surrounding Clwyd Health Authority's refusal to fund Mark's treatment at the Breakspear Hospital, Hemel Hempstead. In January a Daily Mail reader even gave pounds 5,500 to make up the deficit on what Clwyd was prepared to pay - but treatment still could not proceed because of official intransigence.

Last week Clwyd officials broke two months of silence by issuing a press release, explaining their refusal to give the go-ahead. But this contains so many misleading statements that it has provoked a furious response from the Countess of Mar, who regularly embarrasses the government on chemical poisoning issues in the Lords. Last Mar is a victim of similar organo-phosphorous (OP) chemicals to those which destroyed Mark's health when his mother Annette was exposed to them during her pregnancy.

Astonishingly, Clwyd now claims there is 'no evidence' that Mrs Griffin was exposed to OP chemicals by pesticidal spraying in Broughton Hospital, Clwyd, where she worked as a nursing auxiliary in the eighties. Lady Mar points out, in a letter to Mrs Anne Roberts, chairman of Clwyd Health Authority, that Department of Social Security doctors have certified Mrs Griffin as eligible for 'Industrial Injury Benefit C3 (exposure to organo-phosphates)',as a result of her 'exposure to pesticides at work'.

Furthermore, Lady Mar, Clwyd has already accepted responsibility by agreeing to pay for Mrs Griffin and other nurses who worked at

Broughton to be treated at the Breakspear Hospital, widely regarded as Britain's leading centre for treatment of allergies. Mark Griffin has been diagnosed as suffering from chemical poisoning by two leading NHS allergy consultants, who also recommended treatment at the Breakspear. Yet, even more astonishingly, Clwyd now claims the Breakspear is 'not an NHS-recognised hospital'.

Lady Mar points out that the hospital has an NHS Provider Code and that 40 per cent of all its referrals are NHS patients. 'Mrs Griffin,' she adds, 'had not heard of the Breakspear until it was recommended to her by the National Poisons Unit at Guy's Hospital. 'Four Clwyd GPs said they were prepared to refer Mark to the Breakspear, but each time Clwyd removed the family from that doctor's list. Finally Mark was referred by a fifth GP, who a week later was struck off the medical register for other reasons.

Last October, because Mrs Griffin refused to allow Mark to be seen by a Clwyd health authority doctor, moves were made to have the boy taken into care by Clwyd social services. As Lady Mar explains, Mrs Griffin 'sought asylum' by taking Mark to the Breakspear, where she herself was being treated, and where the boy came under the care of hospital director Dr Jean Monro. Clwyd then agreed to fund 'emergency treatment' for the boy, but now claims that, because the Breakspear was 'closed over Christmas for a period of ten days', Mark and his mother had to stay 'in bed and breakfast accommodation' instead of receiving care. Lady Mar, who has been successfully treated at the Breakspear, points out that this accommodation is owned by Dr Monro, under whose care Mark remained throughout that time.

Although the boy was too ill to make another long journey, Clwyd then tried to have the boy seen by Dr Cant, a Newcastle specialist whose expertise does not cover Mark's problems. Dr Cant has told Mrs Griffin that he 'has received no instructions from Clwyd'. In her letter to Clwyd, Lady Mar expresses surprise that Clwyd's chief executive Brian Jones appears to 'have taken upon himself total responsibility' for Mark's case, 'though he is not a clinician'. She ends: 'Unless this situation is resolved immediately I shall have no option but to table an oral question to ask the Minister about the disgraceful way this matter has been handled.'

* * *

In May 1997 a new government was to come into power and with it, a new MP for this constituency. Betty Williams had campaigned for years in local elections. Hoping I might get some representation previously denied me in all the directions in which I had needed to turn, the health authority local council, legal system, social services, I put my needs once more into writing, hoping this time for a less indifferent or dismissive response. But I was to be denied this once again, finally writing to the editor of the newspaper. It was inevitably not to be printed.

As the new prime minister himself and his wife were both lawyers, I was urged the following winter to write to Cherie Blair. From her I did get a sympathetic response, and a kind one. Writing back I nevertheless asked, could she answer the request in the final end of my letter?

To this I had another reply from her secretary saying she was sorry I had been disappointed with her answer, but she had so many letters like mine in effect.

* * *

I had ended my letter with an extract from The Gate of Remembrance which I had learnt of in the autobiography of Michael Bentine, now out of print. The excavation of two chapels at Glastonbury, the Edgar and Loretto chapels had brought about the writing of this book in which are these words:

'Still small voices through the mists of Time, stirring through the void with faint resonances within the deeps of our own Being. . . . the true Communion of the Mind the gate of the Knowledge, whose key is mental sympathy, the key that the lawyers took away, neither entering there, nor permitting others to enter.'

As one who has undertaken to enter the profession of the law, I write to you pleading the recovery of this key. Then I may be able to find comfort in the remaining words:

'No discord can mar this communion, since Love and Understanding are its Law. Death cannot touch it: rather is He Keeper of the Gate. Time, as we know it, here counts for nought, for to the deeper consciousness, a day may be as a thousand years, and a period of trance or sleeping as one tick of the clock.'

I was grateful to receive the sympathy that was sent to me, but had regrettably to accept that it would be no more.

* * *

The home visits from the library service had resumed in the months I had now been living here, and Heddwen Roberts came with books under her arm, and asked me, "How are you?" Then she bent down and laid one of the books she was carrying into my lap, placing it on the flat of her hand. Its title, 'The Family Story' was that of Lord Tom Denning.

Speaking of his schooldays, he described his headmaster, who also taught them cricket, 'he taught us how to keep a straight bat,' he says, and 'how to play the game in life'.

And of an occasion when William Temple went to address a gathering of lawyers at the Inns of Court and opened his remarks by saying, 'I can't say that I know much about law, having been far more interested in justice.

'This supposed division between law on the one hand and morals on the other has been a great mistake,' he writes.

* * *

To:
The Editor,
Pionier Newspaper,
22 Penrhyn Road,
Colwyn Bay
16th May 2000

Dear Editor,

Your newspaper of May 10th reports that Betty Williams MP has had a meeting with the West Wales ME Association. I have lived with this disease undiagnosed for years of my life, since the end of my childhood in fact, until 1987, when the denial of recognition from then on meant more and more brokenness through the critical time of the twelve and a half years since.

The circumstances that beset someone with this kind of condition, that follows a course of incessant relapse and agonising recovery, trying to live through each successive interval while suffering the increasing wrongs of the welfare system, medical comments, and the cumulative consequences, leave the life of someone who has gone through many years of this consummately broken

To have met the refusal of this woman to even look into things has left me utterly devastated. Mrs Betty Williams has received the best of health care treatment herself in having a spinal operation. My critical needs in looking into the health authority, and all the travesty of these years and then the dismissal of Mr David Hardie have received utter denial by her I deserved Mr Hardie's concern, and yet the Community Health Council refused the meeting he tried to arrange.

The grief I have gone through with the social services she would not look into. The council housing benefit office she would not. The loss of a home, and all that went with that home were not her concern. Nor the mistrusted home-care involvement. The legal system through which it happened she did not wish to know. Like the granite this land is made of her refusal was as hard and had as much severity.

I give no name to this letter, but Mrs Williams will recognise to whom such mourning has come.

The well-known lines have many times been written: "*I may but pass this way once in my lifetime... any kindness that I can show to any human being, let me do it now... for I may not have this chance again*"

No words do Justice to the disillusionment, loss of hope, or promise, nor the broken-hearted injury which remains.

15. Diary Of Loss

6th October 1997

This week is little Alexandra's sixth birthday. I remember my own birthday when I was six years old. On October 30th two years ago, my brother entered with the police followed by Mrs Eileen Kemish to whom he had handed photographs taken on her fourth birthday to show to me while he emptied the house.

The police officer had called up his sergeant who also arrived and I explained I was prepared to let my brother take half the contents he wished to remove. Their wish was to send him back to Devon. I regretted I did not allow this. Solicitor Peter Brown would make no contact with me then nor later about this violation of how the decease of my mother should have been handled. Neither they, nor I, nor Mrs Joy Johnson who delivered a faxed copy of my letter to my father's firm, British Aerospace, sent that morning, were able to get a response from the firm, J.W. HUGHES. This intransigence remained throughout the whole two years in which I was unable to find another solicitor willing to take this case on, as John Blakesley had relinquished it.

My request that Peter Brown finally elicit from my brother those belongings he wished to claim, and which he would not consult with me about was accompanied by an inventory of furniture. It did not itemise individual things, nor intimate possessions of mine, ultimately taken, with the help of the home-care woman whose house he used on the various visits he made. Also with the help of a man in the neighbourhood to whom he had also given keys, Mr Chappell.

This diary of loss names these things, essentially intrinsic, valued for the meaning they held, the moment to moment incidents of our lives, domestic and personal, and the memories, some of them of earliest recall, even *before* He was born.

* * *

The 13th October 1996 was the day I learned that the desecration of the Home's repossession included all these belongings. And the things remaining to be cleared in near derelict condition in the garage, due to the winter damage from the burst water tank.

The first things I had thought of were my mother's blue brocade curtains, stored in the loft and made by her so many years before. These I had laundered and they were hung at the window. Next the new material for the side window. It was gone, but the blue brocade had been taken down, clearly at the time the new couple had moved in five days before.

The second bedroom curtains had also been taken down. In the kitchen, however, I had had new William Morris honeysuckle to replace the frayed and very loved linen curtains I was with care relining and mending. At the side window to keep out the draught were the crimson velvet curtains and, standing to the side, the figure of our 'little man', axe in hand (my father had made him a new one), who had stood in our garden from the first days I remembered, in my first home.

Likewise, the bedroom furniture of my mother's, and the downstairs settee and chairs, the window sill vases, and other particularly loved ornaments, were agonizingly gone.

From the sideboard I had taken and wrapped other loved things,

STATEMENT OF CASE: ROSEBAY WILLOW HERB

for the day my brother would come to collect the dining room table, chairs and bookcase/bureau, tea set, and some of the drinking glasses I felt would be reasonably welcome. However, the rest of the furniture was that purchased when my mother and father were married in 1940.

He had taken all of this including the standard lamp, both bookcases, mirrors pictures, and the framed Invocation on the sitting room wall, 'Go, placidly amid the noise and haste, and remember what peace there may be found...'

My mother had framed this prayer two years after I first visited them here, in a picture frame she had bought for my birthday.

The radiogram cabinet had gone and the music records in it. Together with them was the book, *Ill-met By Moonlight* which I had put there as my mother and father's signature-tune which I chose when the commemorative arrangements were being made to celebrate the anniversary of the ending of the War.

There was much-loved, much-played music in that cabinet, much of which was already gone and which I did not know by whom taken. The home-care woman had known 'nothing about it,' as with other things, while she was there in those four years.

My own personal records were also taken, and unbelievably my own gramophone, stored with my things in the garage until division of the contents had reasonably been made and those waiting to be bought into the house had room.

The small worktable that had held sewing things and embroidery silks, I had cherished to keep myself, the chiming clock on the alcove shelf.

When the china rosebud bowl had been taken after my mother's funeral service, I was told by Alma (who brought me home, and who knew, evidently, my brother's intention to return to the home for a 'keepsake') to pack anything precious and she and her husband would mind them. Three months later they brought these back. Easter came and the anniversaries it held. For safekeeping at home, I repacked my grandmothers blue-and-gold teapot, china shell-dish given to my mother by old Mr Oliya, I know, when I was about eight, Mrs Wright's father, next door to us.

The cream and gold trifle dish my mother loved for special

occasions the cake stands, tea-plates and cups from a floral set I had also loved as a child, some of them long-since broken, three cups, saucers and tea-plates of my grandmothers crown derby tea-service, and milk jug and sugar bowl (my aunt, I believe, having the other half of the tea-service), granny Curwen's little cut-glass vinegar bottle and the glass sugar sifter, and some of the wine-glasses, half of which I packed for my brother, some remaining to pack. Also the little wooden elephant called Carla Nag after Rudyard Kipling's story, and a pair of silver initialled serving spoons of Sarah Anne Kendal.

My heart broke when I realised my grandmother's beautiful teapot had gone. I loved it. And had looked forward to using it I had promised myself. The cottage teapot I had had on the kitchen window-sill. I was to discover the entire contents of the cupboards gone completely, together with tea-towels, aprons, cutlery, kitchen recipe books, wine-making and preserves, baking things, and contents of the shelves which I had refurbished with jelly I'd made for my mother to come home, from blackberries and apple-windfalls, jars of cinnamon sugar and vanilla.

That washing machine symbolized the meaningful domesticity of home hours, just as the baking, every baking tin gone, rolling pin, flour, sugar-jars of cinnamon and vanillin, the small rolling pin my mother had always kept in the drawer, made for me by my father, again when I was very little to help to do the baking, just as he had made me a miniature set of tools to follow him round with in the garage when I was still only three.

Upstairs, the remaining things, following my brother's violent entry with escorting police, were no more sacrosanct. Some boxed clothing, summer things, and a quilt stored by the wardrobe were left and a box of sewing things, nevertheless gone through, and wrapped into which were a small Victorian jug and fluted square pot. My bedside cupboard, gone through, taking, among other things, two blouses, stationery, and from the drawers, two nightdresses, old and handmade and lavendered by me which were my mothers and which I had kept. These, I knew, were removed by the home-care woman Pat Stock, who must also have been responsible for the missing silver chain I was mystified to have discovered gone, some while before, and a couple of bedside books missing as well.

My mother's couture grey coat and my black one, were gone. Hers bought for my grandmother's funeral and never worn since, and those things of hers I had saved in the front bedroom fitted cupboard, including her wedding shoes. Things of my own, stored there were also gone. A second spare quilt, suitcase, carpet rug, my Tisserand Journals - all of them. Her bedroom suite, post-war. My Dad's gloves, scarf and old dressing-gown, darned many times. These were my memento of him. His clothes my brother had taken after he died, disposed of for whatever money he could redeem them for. For the second time, he had my father's car. Many years previously he acquired our lovely old Wolseley.

Rehearsed time and time again, and witnessed, were the words my mother had so often reiterated, that my brother and I should never have the hard heartedness to bear of what happened through her grandfather's Will. All they were to leave would be equally divided between us.

How did they come to resign a Will that could be interpreted as this one had?

In the garage where my final things were stored, I found everything had gone, and the boxes of sodden books from the bookcase, one chair and table, broken and cracked crockery of the kind clearly only fit to be left to me, and cooker, made room for. There was my fridge. My own small washer was gone, the spare gas cylinder and primus stove with picnic cylinder in the event of winter emergency without electricity, my own cooking-ware, Pyrex casseroles, cutlery and utensils, were gone.

A remaining box of my own books was there, but the writings of a journal I kept were taken. All my mother's diaries from early years were gone. Her writing case. And a shoe-box full of my personal bank statements, and other personal documents, also gone. One mirror remained of mine. Not a picture.

In all my loss when I had first come here to visit my father I, when all my Life contained then, garnered for the meaning of Home, was laid to ashes, I went into the warmth of a tea room one day where I was served by dear Imelda Ward. Kindly enquiring of me whether I was 'visiting', I explained.

She told me that She was to fulfil a lifetime's wish in May to visit Lourdes. 'Write a message,' she said. 'And place with it an offering.'

'I will leave it in the grotto there.'

Above the table was a lovely lampshade of honeysuckle shape and design. I admired it. 'I will make it my gift to you,' she said.

I know not the hearts and minds of those living in the hillside home today. But my lampshade must still hang there.

16. Bioresonance, Burrows Lea & Mr Ng

The descending year reached mid-winter and the darkest days started eventually to lighten again. I thought of wintertime in my childhood and one early morning woke, finding myself running down my garden path at the front of the house to the gate where I had pushed my wooden horse so that I could stand on the carpet seat to chatter to anybody who passed by, going to the shop or post office perhaps or walking their dog. Running, running on my legs now so painful and tired as all my limbs were, and drained, I felt in this dwelling.

Some weeks later a copy of the newsletter from the research network printed a description of bioresonance, a way of measuring the body's own frequencies and those of pathogens that could be attenuated or diminished, and I learnt in detail of scientific studies and treatments going back to the 1960s onwards including bioresonance therapy used in the Russian Space Programme and in most Russian hospitals and ambulances. In 1994 this led to the FDA approving the Sonic Accelerated Fracture Healing System (SAFHS) which emits ultrasound pulses. The mapping of the body's energy patterns and their fine-tuning can be used to benefit the immune system and the resilience to environmental dissonance which tires and depletes the body all the time. I sent for a list of practitioners of this treatment.

To my delight I learnt that my nearest practitioner was in Wistaston, my childhood home, at Wistaston Park, two moments or more from the garden path I had run down in my dream. I was going to go back there. I was going back to get well

I telephoned Andrew Barry and it was arranged that I would go for my first treatment on their return from going away, an arrangement they had planned, but I did not know, with a view to leaving in the imminent future. He told me this first thing when I arrived, but it would take some time he said to sell the house and the possibility lay ahead of treatment, and in my dear hope, some way of going back to live there.

I stood on the railway platform at Penmaenmawr and the mountain, so severe from a distance, looked on with seeming kindness as it had before eleven years ago, when I made my fateful and reluctant journey to see Dr Finn again, and to have all the tests done that he wanted. JourneyCare assistance was given me when I arrived in Chester and had to change trains. I eventually arrived at Crewe. The last time I had been on the station platform here was on a nostalgia visit when my primary school headmaster Mr Platt had seen me off on the train back to Wales within the first two years I had come here to visit the sanatorium in Snowdonia. A taxi took me along the Crewe Road towards Wells Green, turning off down Broughton Lane beforehand and finally into a turning of a few pleasantly spaced bungalows which had been named Wistaston Park.

For an hour and a half I sat with pads across my shoulders, middle and lower back receiving the programmed frequencies to balance and enhance my depleted reserves. But I had the return journey to make. I was kindly taken to the station and another treatment was arranged in a fortnight's time.

Once again I stood on the railway station and slowly round the headland the train pulled along towards the footbridge, and slowly, slowly carried on.

STATEMENT OF CASE: ROSEBAY WILLOW HERB

* * *

At the very end of this long, empty platform it finally came to a stop already past a boarding point. Then, equally as slowly the train moved backwards again until the guard could dismount and call out down the length of the platform, "Are you getting on this train, madam?" I had to point out that it was hardly possible due to the gap between the railway carriage and the sloping end of the platform. So having inched a few yards further back and having put his hand under one elbow and arm under the other, we finally boarded the train together. Jovially he sat opposite me after punching my rail ticket and then went up to the driver's cab. He returned some twenty minutes later and chatted for most of the rest of the way. At Chester however we had drawn up to the wrong platform. All the negotiations had to be made to get transported across the railway line and into the waiting train for Crewe and by the time I reached the front door at Wistaston Park I could hardly step across into the hall. Telling the story of my journey we laughed and Andrew, who had been doing some research, proceeded with the treatment as before.

Despite having arrived so spent of my journey strength, I was feeling on air as I walked out into the garden afterwards. But again, there was the journey back.

The train was crowded this time and I sat in a carriage with a lady getting off at Rhyl. As the train pulled away however, a voice over the tannoy said, "Welcome aboard the train to Carlisle stopping at Warrington..." The lady and I didn't listen to anymore but turned to one another in dismay. Getting up she managed to push her way to the guard and said we had been put on the wrong train at Crewe. In fact the train had divided and we were meant to have been shown into the other half.

At Warrington we disembarked and after a wait of some time a special train was put on to return us, this time to Chester, so that we could get the connecting train back to North Wales.

Getting out at Rhyl, the lady gave me her address and said she would be writing to the railway and would tell them I was returning after some treatment and was not well. I put my key in the door after my second brave attempt to travel a two hour journey to do something, anything, to lessen the ill state I was living through. The treatment had been wonderful, but it had all been in vain.

Andrew had decided it would make me too much worse to instigate detoxifying treatment, especially as I had nobody to look after me. Hence despite his attempt to concentrate on improving my wellbeing, this, my body would not handle. He did, however decide that my next treatment was to be to measure the mercury levels in all my teeth and how many were leaking.

* * *

It is possible through bioresonance technology to send an 'inverse oscillation' pattern of energy of any toxin to the body to cancel out its electromagnetic charge. This renders the toxin inert, or nearly so. With little or no energy in the electromagnetic field, the immune system can then remove toxins from the body. The sequence and order of these therapies are important and must be done with care in order to successfully clean the toxins out of the matrix of the connective tissue.

For example, when you push a child on a swing, the energy of each push adds to the energy of the child swinging and the child swings higher and higher. This is called 'Constructive Interference'. When it's time to stop you push in a way that slows the swing down and stops the 'oscillation' of the swing. This is called in physics 'Destructive Interference' and in bioresonance it is called 'Inverse Oscillation Therapy'. (Ref. The New Hope Clinic a Quantum Wellness Center.)

Despite being an engineer's daughter this science was way beyond my grasp and I only knew that bioresonance could tune our bodies back into harmony and well-being.

I had already had galvanometer readings done by a dentist in Beaumaris whose name had been given to me as a holistic dentist. I needed a replacement filling in an upper right tooth that had long been a troublesome tooth, and he proceeded to put a dressing in the tooth for me without any numbing of my gum before drilling into it. For this I paid one hundred and twenty pounds, knowing that I could not return there.

I arrived in a lot of pain with inflammation in the tooth for my next visit to Wistaston, having been met at Chester with wheelchair assistance after the lady's letter to the railway following the previous journey. After some first-aid bioresonance for this tooth I was able to spend an hour resting in a room looking onto the garden.

I made a fourth visit and Andrew prepared some oil programmed with frequencies that would help my resistance to geopathic stress. The electro-magnetic field of the body, or life-field, is influenced by underground water flows and high voltages from deep underground rock under stress, which travels up rock faults. The energy flows above and below the ground at various levels in narrow river-like patterns that 'home in' on things they are attracted to. Energies may be under the bed where the body repairs its cells while asleep. The Earth's magnetic field produces grid patterns some intersections of which the body will dislike. In those who are ill the body's repair process is prevented by this. And babies are vulnerable to this until their nerve sheathing is fully formed.

During May a barristers' meeting had been arranged in Chester by the now further solicitors meant to be representing me. But it became clear from this stage on that I was never going to be represented in the way they had promised. I decided that it was untenable for me to continue to go through the mind draining business of dealing with solicitors who did not wish to apply their integrity to my case. I had gone back to the solicitors in Conwy after John Blakesley had been granted his leave to remove himself from the Court Record and they had allowed the case to become 'out of time' by doing absolutely nothing at all to help me, and had refused determinedly to go up to the hillside home when the water tank burst or to make any assessment of the damage to my own belongings, nor to that of the home, which was clearly vandalised during the time builders were working on it according to what our hillside neighbour Eileen said. The Chester solicitors, after reassuring me that they were going to look into the Case for Negligence that had been proposed by Michael Baker in 1991, instead cancelled my certificate with the Legal Aid Board that had been obtained under the Inheritance Act in 1995.

My Appeal Hearing was with the help of St. John's Ambulance once again who unhesitatingly took me in to Chester. The chairman was Mr Mike O'Connor who, with his other two colleagues, was of the view that I would not want to go on with solicitors that had let me down in this way. I said of course, "No," but they said they could not advise about where I should turn for further legal help. I should write to the Lord Chancellor, Lord Irvine. In just under an hour I left, knowing my certificate would be re-instated, but it arrived without delay with the provision that proceedings had to be served on the Trustees within five weeks. Five weeks! I was spent with the number of times I had had to try and get further legal help. The case had become too convoluted for other solicitors to have the time to take it on. Especially after Edwards Hughes in Colwyn Bay, and David Jones had allowed the unlawful repossession of my rooms up the mountain at Craig Lwyd Hall and inserted a note in my file enclosing a missionary leaflet with the illustration of a tiger and the caption, 'alright, alright, I know there aren't any lions in the jungle, but I've only got a picture of a tiger so let's pretend.'

After returning from the barristers meeting in May I telephoned the Legal Aid Board and told them I was withdrawing from any further attempts to get the representation I deserved. They did not, however, cancel my Legal Aid certificate for another whole year, by which time, no fee had been presented. A sum of money was proposed for compensation for loss and damage to my belongings, but not for loss nor damage to me. I refused. This did not compensate me for such lack of Duty of Care.

Costs were awarded to the Trustees and the hillside home sold for a song. Insurance had been claimed for winter flooding from the burst water tank during the time I was in lodgings. A sum of money then remained in a Life Trust for myself with a clause that any monies needed by myself should be made available by the Trustees at their discretion in time of need.

I stayed the night in Wistaston on having my treatment before this barristers meeting. Andrew and his wife, Anne, said a farewell to me in the morning, their home having been sold sooner than they had expected. And I had not, after all, been able to return there, to Wistaston, and to the well-being of my dream.

**

Leighton Hospital, near Crewe, had done the blood tests for the mercury and the nickel in my teeth, to which I had a high sensitivity as well. There was no further treatment for bioresonance for this. I had the decision to make about finding a dentist to replace my fillings with white ones. It was a darker and more cavernous nightmare into which I felt I could not go, and into which I should not have gone. Another twelve months later I was told, when every filling of amalgam had been replaced, that I would need three monthly visits, and I had spent money, back-dated for medical benefit, to have them done. And I had to spend as much again, for the mineral syrups and drops, to bind the free-flowing mercury now in my blood and all the withdrawal which was to go on for years. I had pain in the bone, hip joint, and sores on the ends of my toes for four winters. My temperature dropped and I shivered all day every day, unable to keep warm. It was, I learnt, adrenal collapse.

I had made contact again with Burrows Lea and with the Sanctuary, in whose healing thoughts and prayers I was held, from then on.

My mother had written to Burrows Les and Harry Edwards to ask for healing for the baby girl of her dear friend, Eunice, and I saw for myself the healing work for which he was such a wonderful channel at a demonstration of healing in Woking a few years later. In the parting 'goodbyes' as he made his way to leave that evening, he took both my hands in his. His blessing came to return to me as I lived through these years so long afterwards. I felt the deepest sadness when Ray and Joan Branch, who carried on the healing work at the Sanctuary for so many years themselves, departed, and the many changes that have taken place since. Jean and Vincent Hill still carried on, Vincent having been born and spent his boyhood at Burrow Lea. Today, Jean is still there, and the thoughts and prayers that have sustained me, gave great relief to the pain I suffered when first recovering from the surgery to my eye five years later.

As another winter drew on towards spring I continued to endure the sense of confinement with unlessened yearning to find some kind of wings like the little bird that landed on the hedge outside my narrow kitchen window and then took off again with the lightness and freedom I wished were my gift. With laboured steps I could walk to the post office at St Gwynans a little way up the hill. But not with the legs I used to take our sheepdog up to the waterfall. They were legs I was not to have again. I managed one day, but once only, to get as far as the bus stop to get on the bus into Conwy. I got off at the top of the town and walked down under the archway to the Square, and then, decidedly, I walked into the post office and asked for a driving license form.

* * *

The challenge to drive again after 26 years was more than unnerving. When eventually I came to have a second hand Ford car I was to find myself with nerve pain in my hands and fingers just from turning the steering wheel, and my rib cage and stomach felt the immense effort of negotiating any turn. But it was a liberation I had to persevere to regain. Long months would elapse when I could not drive at all. But I thought constantly of the little bird, and I thought of the journeys I might eventually be able to make.

I thought of the mill at Sedgeberrow, just outside Evesham, the village where I had been befriended by Siam and Emrys. Emrys I knew, had collapsed suddenly on stage at a performance at the Chichester theatre. I had learnt this while living up the mountain in those years of isolation when the wireless was most of the time, my only contact with the outside world.

When I was given the dwelling here, I listened to a broadcast of Sian's first book, *A Small Country*, which had been dramatised for radio, and knew she had moved back to Dyfed. It had taken much enquiry to learn what had happened to Raymond Shaw, who had lived at the mill. And it was with much sadness that I was eventually to know he had had to move into the village of Elmley Castle and sell the mill, having become ill with Parkinson's disease. Would I ever, I wondered, be able to drive down there and find him. He needed taking care of I was certain. He had had to move into the mill after having to sell his mother's cottage to repair the roof. He was lost so much after she died, this was a terrible blow to him! The water board had diverted the stream and he lost the case over being unable to prevent them, and had to pay the costs. It was therefore no longer a working mill. The tragedy of this seemed to me insensible. Why lose this water power, such a valuable resource?

He was asked if he could lay a new floor upstairs at the Almonry in the square in Evesham, but the cost of elm had gone up during the winter and he had been ill. He had lost £300 because of the increase in the price of timber.

I had taken my father to see him and to see the mill when they came down to visit me and in my father he found like-minded company. He came out of his shy, retiring shell on a visit he then made up to North Wales and was persuaded to stay the night. I had written to tell him when my father had died. There had been no reply. Now I understood why.

My father's skilled background in engineering meant he took an experienced interest in the workings of the mill which were now so still and silent. I wonder, who became the owner? Would the government ever take steps to allow it to become a working mill again?

I wanted to return there. I wanted to know. I wanted to find Raymond Shaw in all his sad state, no doubt reclusive as before. He had called out to me, friendly and invited me to look at the swallows, that first day I walked past. They were darting in and out of the loft, the doors wide open letting in the first sun of that cold spring. He would walk over the fields with Molly, his dog, and come back and make warm soup for both of them on his aga cooker, removed from an old house, which he had managed to install. He and Molly shared their meals, both confirmed vegetarians. His mother's clothes hung from the rafters on coat hangers, and a few trinkets of hers he kept in a bowl. I must find out what had happened to him now.

* * *

The challenge of the days ahead were to lengthen into the years ahead however, and I was not to have the wings I needed, and that I yearned for. Ill winters followed by spring I could not enjoy, and summer days that were stressful, and lessened only in passing during the weeks of autumn when some replenishment and calm gained a presence.

I wished that spring and autumn were not so passing, the first flush of spring especially seemed to be passed so fleetingly and I would feel the increasing tension in the earth as spring became summer and I failed to keep up with Mother Nature's fast burgeoning. It would just leave me in grief, and I wanted countryside in which I could feel refreshed not lonely, not desolate, but in harmony with my surroundings.

Each year disappointed me. I would look ahead, thinking, *this time next year I shall be better than I am*, and I would bless the land I thought

I was going to leave. Whatever significance it may have had, if any, I shall never know. But my link with this mountain, I knew without a doubt, would never be broken. Wherever its granite was taken in the world, for whatever road building purposes, it would spread 'light paths' and that essence of the 'love ray'. In the world where conflict only seemed to increase and where suffering among all the creature kingdoms as well as humankind and the innocent abounded, I could only pray that my mountain would mother this suffering.

In the passing of each year, my own grief did not lessen. I continued to take the mineral syrups and drops to clear my system of the harmful residues from the removal of my fillings. This had all been to help my immune system to re-gather some sustainable level of living with this condition. But now I was having streamers suddenly down my eye. It followed a visit I had had from my brother. He had suddenly announced he wished to visit me. And now what looked like dark red streamers were flowing down my eye, blurring wholly my vision, I wasn't able to keep my balance properly and tiredness had completely overtaken me as I went to lie down. At the end of that afternoon I got up to make some tea to drink, but could not see properly to pour the water from the kettle into the cup, I went to bed no better and on waking the next morning, I was frightened to know what had happened. I went to the telephone and rang the emergency out of hours telephone number. Within twenty minutes ambulance men were at the door to take me to the A&E department of Glan Clwyd Hospital. The sister, Sister Mair in A&E had said, "The trouble is that we live in a triangle between Sellafield in Cumbria Wylfa power station on Anglesey, and Trawsfynydd in mid-Wales." Even though Trawsfynydd is decommissioned it will take another forty years for the radiation to diminish. Now an open Nature Trail Trawsfynydd has a visitor centre.

My bioresonance had cleared my system of fall-out from Chernobyl five years before which had been measured on the beaches at Llanfairfechan. The Sister switched off the lights in the cubicle for me as I lay waiting after drops had been put into my eye, The long morning passed and after being seen by the Asian doctor on duty, she said to me that I had had a severe vitreous haemorrhage and would have to go to the Eye Hospital at St Asaph, H.M. Stanley and in this knowledge that yet another journey would have to be made, I was taken back and kindly seen indoors to spend the hours until morning. It had been a Sunday. It had been my birthday.

* * *

I had just come through my eighth winter in this dwelling here, the half-way house I thought it was to have been. Lonely desolation, grief, anguish, the sum of years, had caught up with me. It had been towards that fourth winter, the end of autumn, when the constant thought of the little girl, now nearing her eighth birthday, made me decide to write to her. I sent to her the story of the children in Yorkshire who had taken photographs with an old camera they had been given, of the beck where they used to go and play. They had, they said, seen fairies, and photographed them. Arthur Conan Doyle had taken an interest in the children. The story had formed a book written by Geoffrey Hodgson which I had had many years before. I learnt it had been made into a film. I sent a letter saying that she had once visited me when she was a baby and she would have been too tiny to remember, but that I remembered, and thought about her often. I wished for her a happy birthday.

My brother replied saying would I confirm my address. I then received a brief note and a card from her enclosing her photograph. Not long afterwards I received a letter from my brother again. He had upgraded his instructor status for flying. He was working for a company called Channel Express. Cards and messages continued from time to time. She said she would visit. Her next birthday came and went. And her next. And I realised the novelty of making a visit to Wales had worn off. My brother said it was too far for her to come. He sent some photographs taken that Christmas at Disney Land in France.

His notification that he wanted to make a visit came out of the blue. He was flying to Liverpool airport. He wanted to go somewhere for lunch.

I could not have felt more ill as I got ready in my coat for when he arrived. He said straight away, could we go into Conwy and we spent the hour of his visit in the Clemence restaurant. He talked mainly of Alexandra, of what she was doing and that she wanted to be a journalist. Then he said it was all the news he had, and asked if I was ready to go. We drove back up and onto the pass and I knew there were rivers and streamers running down my eye of dark red. At the door he said, "Goodbye." I could barely see him. He tooted as he drove the car away. I lay down, every feeling cauterised. I could not bear to feel any more of the pain in mind and heart I had known. It had worn me to this, by days, nights and years, and bewilderment for some kind of meaning was all that remained.

* * *

At the hospital the next day on Sunday morning I had drops in my eyes as soon as I arrived and twenty minutes later was taken into the darkened room where my eye was examined by Mr Ng. There was too much blood for him to 'see anything'. I was to return in a week. By this time I was too frightened to go back and telephoned Mrs Irene Gameson, a former radiologist at the Royal Free Hospital and who kept a blind shop behind the chemist owned by Mr Evans. In 1944 she had been one of the many nurses and staff at the hospital who suffered from an outbreak of what later became known as ME but at that time named Royal Free Disease. Later in a paper written by Alf Riggs, specialist in Telluric radiation, he maintained the cause of this to be the underground flow of the River Fleet beneath the nurses dormitories in Fleet Street, water giving off a very high voltage or radiation under pressure, as does underground rock.

Irene Gameson told me I must follow everything the hospital told me at all costs. Her husband had had a haemorrhage as severe, and was a professional mountaineer. He had gone back to climbing and lost his full sight as a result. She had kept the blind shop ever since. She had a folder full of information and research into ME and knew the full implications for me. As my eye became more painful I rang the RNIB. They said the bleeding would continue, and the pain would get worse. I had to go back. It would not be possible just to manage with my remaining sight. Both eyes were joined to the one optic nerve.

I had never ever taken my sight for granted and considered it always a gift for which I was grateful. At the hospital when I was taken again I was told I was to be operated upon on Thursday of that week. It had reached Easter and it was Maundy Week.

I was collected at ten past seven in the morning. I was told I must have nothing to eat or drink after five o'clock, but I drank some tea.

Without this I could not face the day to come. There was the keenest frost and on getting out of the hospital car it cut into me, and into my eye. The anaesthetist came to see me and all the necessary preparations were made, and then I was taken into the side room to the theatre. This is where they stood with face masks prepared to put the syringe into my hand. I was by now petrified beyond bearing. The knowledge that there was a fifty percent chance of failure or success intensified every other unhappiness I had lived with during years of loss. Forefront of it all, the loss and absence of the dearest love that I needed every day and the fortitude I had to find to live, missing this.

A nurse woke me at exactly twenty-five past two. My head throbbed with an arc of pain right across the top of my head where I felt my head must have been held in some kind of clamp, and my throat and the roof of my mouth felt raw. My eye was covered up, but the nurse let up the blinds, and with my other eye I could see!

I was asked would I eat a piece of toast and drink a cup of tea. I said I could not eat the toast, but I needed the tea. I was wheeled into the recovery area which was spacious and comfortable, and without any delay my transport arrived to bring me back. In the days following I saw everything in a kind of 3D as drops had been put into my eye to keep the iris wide open. I watched a bee in the honeysuckle, flowering in the first warming days of spring. Everything had a kind of ethereal hue for those few days, until the magic began to fade. As I looked into the mirror, I thought, *what a marvel the gift of sight is!* And gratitude for that never left me from then on. In the corridor of the hospital when I returned for the dressing to be taken off the next day, I was able to read all the cards and messages of relief and thanks from those who had been operated upon the previous week. For the gifted dexterity and fine precision with which my operation had been done, I remained permanently thankful. I was told a letter would be sent to my optician, Melvyn Hughes in Conwy, and on my visit to him that followed, I said all this. I said I had asked a nurse beforehand if I could possibly see any kind of video film showing how the operation would be done, and the nurse had looked horrified! He said he had attended one of Mr Ng's lecture training demonstrations, but that much of it was very advanced for him to follow. The hospital had been there for five years, he said, having moved to North Wales from Liverpool. They were at the cutting edge.

My brother continued to write from time to time, or to send a card from wherever he was flying. For a time his location was on the Isle of Man and he would write saying he was flying over Snowdonia. In 2009 the airfield was sold and he had to deliver his aircraft to East Africa to Dar Es Salam flying to eight other airfields altogether on the way. It was a journey, he wrote, into the unknown.

There would be the promise of a visit when Alexandra had done her end of term exams. The year would pass, the next and the next, and then she was learning to drive. They would come up to North Wales through the forest. Her exams were taken again at the end of an extended year and she moved to university. A card written the next year told me she was spending her second twelve months in Australia.

I had no longer continued to write to her after her sixteenth birthday. I decided to send the Life Story of Lady Muriel Dowding for this final gift as it also portrayed the beliefs and the principles by which I myself had lived. In November my brother wrote to say the book had been passed onto her, but there had been no reply from herself. When home during the holidays she lived with her mother in Taunton. He sent cards from Germany where he was by then working from an airfield at Friedrichschafen on the borders of Austria and said she was going out there to spend Christmas and to go skiing. Each letter or card that came I knew furthered the distance of their lives from my own, and I wished them well, my brother especially, in that he seemed intrinsically lonely, despite his full and time-filled lifestyle.

In time I was to start to suffer a blurring in my eye, and was told this was inevitable, and that they would never be able to operate on the same eye twice. So this was the cost I was to have to face for hours of crying, sometimes on the floor, because of a legal travesty and the ruthlessness I just could not understand, that had brought it all about.

* * *

Since then I have not been able to help looking back and thinking that if keyhole surgery had been available years and years ago, I would never have lost the dearest love, that left me bereft and wandering as these years have been since, nor would I have been diminished by this legal system under which we have to live.

17. Final Days

In the meantime a summer went on, the first flush of spring over, the days once again became a strain as geopathic stress increased its effect especially when sleeping, and I knew that every day the rock was being blasted on the mountain, just as it had been blasted out to make the two tunnels on the A55 when this road building had begun back in 1986, the same year as the Chernobyl disaster. Sometimes I would feel the bed vibrate two thirds of the way down. I would think that a train must he passing through but it would go on for twenty minutes or so, then rest, then start again. I suffered the worst headaches that summer, of any, and then it was announced in August, my worst month, that there had been more sunspots that summer than for 100 years. I knew, however, that there were some who suffered much worse, and could not go out in daylight. It was a relief when September came, and a quieting and still time in the days gave them restfulness.

It was a sudden and emotional shock, then to get a brief message saying that my brother wanted to visit me with Alexandra in two days time. I had had to find in some way a transcending of the clear knowledge that I was no part of her life, and that my brother's life of travel would never include visiting me again, and to find an inner sustainment. I was held in the thoughts of those at Burrows Lea and the Sanctuary and their healing thoughts had helped me through my frightening time at the eye hospital and afterwards.

I decided to ring and I found myself talking to Jean Hill. She said, "Well I think you are just not well enough for a visit like this."

She more than knew it was the truth, but I said, "Do you think I could find the grace to let them come."

I spoke briefly to my brother who said they would be on their way back to University. I spent the next forty eight hours, shaking and drinking warm oat milk to cope with the shock to my system after all these years of so much emotional pain. The morning came of their arrival and I decided to phone and find out when they would be here. They were the other side of Llangollen, he said, and would arrive just after twelve. I had decided to ring the bakery and ask for a table for some kind of lunch which they would be wanting. I knew in their kindness they would not hesitate.

It was some two hours later that the phone rang, and it was her voice. They were 'running late.' It was all she said. Nothing more.

Eventually at nearly twenty to two I thought I had better ring the bakery and let them know that they had never arrived. They would have saved a table specially. I had been sinking long enough and I could not go on, and trembling, as I spoke to them, my brother was suddenly waving and coming down the garden path.

Reaching the door he greeted me, and said, "This is Alexandra."

*　*　*

There was nothing of his warm greeting in her response, however. Nothing more distant could there have been in her 'hello'. Since leaving Llangollenthey they had decided to tour Snowdonia so that she should see something of North Wales. They had clearly stopped for some refreshments along the way for she only toyed with soup and a bread roll while my brother drank a pot of coffee. They had been driving, he said, since quarter past six. There was no concept of how weakening the morning's wait had been made for me. Nor, in fact, the news that they were coming, after the long ill time I had had.

STATEMENT OF CASE: ROSEBAY WILLOW HERB

Sitting at the table, she told me of her end of year results and her plan to take her university degree in *philosophy* and politics. She mentioned her mother. 'She was a criminal lawyer...'

***

Leaving my stomach hollow, we made to leave, my brother choosing some cakes to take back with them. I thanked the bakery for their trouble and on the way out she turned to me and said, "Did he tell you he lost his passport in Germany?" I said he had lost his passport in Belgium many years before when he was quite young and had been helped by the British Embassy to get back home. There had been a letter from the Consul to my parents in reply to a letter of thanks for their help at the bureau. On the way back to the car he bought me a new toaster as I mentioned I needed one. He had been saying to her while we had sat at the table, was there anything she needed in the house she was going to share for her last year at university. She had said she needed some pans and cutlery.

"I've got plenty of cutlery, you can have some of mine!" The words went on and on in my mind in many nights to follow.

She wanted postcards to take back of Llanberis Pass, but we looked in vain. My brother wanted to take a photograph in the front garden before they left. He kissed me goodbye and they went. And my heart turned over, knowing that, never would they come again. That it was a once and only visit, and despite their words, their lives would take over any intention of their returning would be a lost memory. Time would not be a long lonely heartache for them. Their time would be filled, fully and complete.

Not long went by when I received a card from my brother saying 'thank you' for the visit. He was doing further training on a simulator so that he could instruct students on the flight deck of a Boeing 747. During the autumn and winter he stayed with a friend in the forest while training and working. But I received nothing from her, not even on sending some reprints of old photographs she had asked for, nor even to say that money for her birthday had been received. At Christmas I received a card, also some slippers and an acknowledgement. Two weeks into the New Year I was to have a road accident and no reserves in me with which to make recovery from the trauma of it for months on, into another year.

I was driven back by the driver of the car behind me who witnessed the signal wrongly given by the van driver that he was turning left into the road at the end of which we were waiting. I had pulled a few feet forward and he had carried on, smashing my headlamp and leaving me shattered behind the wheel.

"Is there anyone I could contact?" she wanted to know. Her sister and mother had been in the car she was driving.

"No," I said, "I just need to lie down."

But she insisted. "There must be somebody." She would not go and leave me unless there was someone for whom she could send.

My brother was in Germany. He had bought somewhere to live for himself while based at Friedrichschafen, which he now needed to sell. He answered his phone when she rang him however. A few days later he rang up to see how I was. He asked about the slippers and whether I had received them. I sent a note to be forwarded on to her and mentioned I was getting over a road collision... I received a visit from the community police, several in fact... My headlamp was repaired in two days, but I wasn't.

A few weeks later, just after Easter at the beginning of April, my elderly neighbour died. She was suddenly and sadly taken very ill and her strong constitution took its leave and surgery left her on a Care Pathway. Knowing this made it impossible to spend any more nights in the bedroom. It was more than I could bear. I had known her to be the last of many relatives who had died before her including her husband who had died on her birthday, as my father had done on my mother's. Despite her age she had gone out in the early mornings on Friday of each week to get the bus to the hospital in her WVS uniform until she was eighty four, as my aunt had done. Her memory today remains undiminished.

My brother rang again in May and knew I was upset. He would ring again he said. The weeks passed by and most of the summer. I started to wonder if anything was wrong. He had had a sore throat when he phoned previously. He could just be busy. But eventually I thought of the possibility that he might have had a bee sting. He would not have reacted well to this! I decided to ring and find out.

Oh.... He had been busy! He had been building an extension to the dining room of a house he had built in his garden… of which I had not had any idea. The couple living there had found it too small.

* * *

I could only think of the mill at Sedgberrow and Raymond Shaw with sad regret that another summer had passed now, and that what strength I had in the day was spent with every little effort. No sustainability had I to think of a long drive. Even to go into Conwy I had taken Castle Cabs or Elwyn's. In a few weeks more the bed of winter would have come and I would be spending it by dimmed lamplight which I had to switch out early. And there would come the end of another year, that I had lived in this dwelling here. I should wait for bulbs to come up for another spring, snowdrops, and tie tincture of propolis on some tree bandage to wrap round the bark of my old little apple tree, that would bear blossom again in the warmer days when they arrived. The grass would be cut and the first sweet smell of it would fill the air. Grace, my elderly neighbour would have been out in her garden, and her washing would blow, billowing below cumulus clouds, and the first bumblebees would remind me once again of those four and five days when I saw the world as a bee does with that luminous insight into each flower. These were the only things upon which to dwell to bear the undercurrent; of heartache. And think of the future wishes for where I should lie when the time came that Mother Earth gave me my last home.

* * *

Up on the hillside where lambs and daffodils were the scene of the day there are now a sea of roofs, a small green with oaks, a waterfall, and a once patch of waste ground apposite one of the rows of hillside homes, now also built upon. There grew the abundance one summer of Rosebay Willow-Herb that Mother Nature had sown in her wise way, with its butterflies and moths, There, in her waste place did she beautify that unwanted land.

The line of trees on the edge of the verge are gone now, the beautiful ash, and the rest. They lie now in Mother Nature's memory. And she will show her wild seed somewhere else.

There is a Celtic legend of the Morrigan who kneels at the riverside at the world's ends and washes the stains from our clothing. And a ferryboat man to row us across to the other side when our life here is done.

Oh, Ferry me across the water, do boatman do,
If you've a penny in your purse, I'll ferry you.
I have a penny in my purse, and my eyes are blue,
So ferry me across the water, do, boatman do.

Step into my ferryboat, be they black or blue,
And for the penny in your purse, I'll ferry you.

Printed in Great Britain
by Amazon.co.uk, Ltd.,
Marston Gate.